JOHN MAGEZI

SPIRITUAL
LAWS

The Operating System of the Kingdom of God

TATE PUBLISHING & *Enterprises*

Published by Tate Publishing & Enterprises, LLC
127 E. Trade Center Terrace | Mustang, Oklahoma 73064 USA
1.888.361.9473 | www.tatepublishing.com

Tate Publishing is committed to excellence in the publishing industry. The company reflects the philosophy established by the founders, based on Psalm 68:11,
"The Lord gave the word and great was the company of those who published it."

Book design copyright © 2011 by Tate Publishing, LLC. All rights reserved.
Cover design by Kellie Southerland
Interior design by Lindsay B. Behrens

Published in the United States of America

ISBN: 978-1-61777-383-9
1. Religion / Christian Life / General
2. Religion / Christian Life / Spiritual Growth
11.03.31

Table of Contents

Introduction

Manufacturers all over the world issue manuals, alongside their products, to their customers. These booklets, usually called "owner's manuals," are intended to provide basic operation guidelines for these products.

They are also intended to ensure the safety and longevity of these products. Adherence to the advice provided in these manuals would not only result in the optimum performance of these products, but also in their durability. Conversely, negligence or ignorance of these guidelines could result in not only minimal performance of the products, but also in their frequent breakdowns and short lifespan.

In the same way, God, the Master Creator, has issued guidelines for the optimum performance and longevity of his creation. He has put in place both physical and spiritual laws to enable man enjoy "abundant life."

Disobedience of these guidelines by the first man, Adam, together with his wife, Eve, greatly reduced man's lifespan on the earth. Man shifted from an opportunity to live forever to only a few years on the earth. With the increase of sin on the face of the earth, these years even became less and less, until we see them at eighty years in the scriptures—see Psalm 90, verse 10.

In this book, I discuss what I call *spiritual laws*. These are principles God has given us to enable us to live a fruitful and long life. God says he wants us to have "life and life more abundantly" (see John chapter 10, verse 10). God has given us not only commandments to obey, but also principles to live by.

In the book of Isaiah the Bible says, "…for my thoughts are not your thoughts, neither are your ways my ways saith the Lord. For as the heavens are higher than the earth so are my ways higher than your ways and my thoughts than your thoughts" (Isaiah 55:8–9).

What God is simply saying here is that his way of doing things is different from the way people normally do things. God is also saying that his way of doing things is superior to the way of man. This means you get better results if you do things God's way. God's way is the best way you can do something. You get more satisfaction if you do things God's way.

Spiritual laws are spiritual principles God has put in place to guide his creation into a more productive life. They are God's "operating system" or his "modus operandi." They initially affect our status in the spiritual realm, but later the consequences are evident in the physical realm.

For something to qualify as a law, it must always have similar consequences, provided certain things remain constant. With a law, therefore, one can accurately predict the outcome of certain actions. God has put in place certain laws or principles that would have a similar outcome in the same environment.

The discovery of physical laws by the world of science and technology has led to outstanding innovations, which have revolutionized the lives of many people. We have heard of the law of gravity, the law of thermodynamics, etc., in the world of physics.

Man has been able to go to the moon, to fly in the air like the birds, and to manufacture all sorts of wireless gadgets as a result of the discovery of these laws.

These breakthroughs have been duplicated all over the world by following the same laws. So we have cars made in Japan and others made in Germany all following the same dynamics or laws.

In the same way for the church to get mighty breakthroughs in the spiritual realm, we must discover and operate God's spiritual laws. These laws are applicable anywhere in the world provided certain things are the same.

The ignorance or the negative application of these laws always has dire consequences. Many people are living life at a minimum for failure to positively apply these laws.

Spiritual laws not only reveal God's "operating system," they also reveal his impartiality in dealing with man. The Bible says that God is no "respecter of persons," meaning that God does not show any unqualified favoritism. He has given all of us the same set of laws, thus giving all of us an equal opportunity to succeed in life.

God, by giving us these laws, has not left us in the dark. He has enlightened us on the best way to live our life in this world. It's now up to us to take heed to his advice and reap the harvest that comes with it.

Even though I know that the laws discussed in this book are not the total sum, they will go a long way to enlighten us about a good number of them. These laws, though closely related, have significant differences that are worth examining.

Law of Thought

"As a man thinketh in his Heart so is he" (Proverbs 23:7).

The first law I would like to discuss in this book says that a person becomes like what he thinks. This law is found in Proverbs 23 verse 7. This law says, basically, that you will eventually become what you think about. You will turn out to be like your dominant thoughts.

Thoughts are not innocent, powerless, harmless things, as we sometimes believe. If they take root, they are powerful vehicles for change. The Bible says that thoughts have transforming power.

We are told in the Bible not to be conformed to the patterns of this world but to be "... transformed by the renewing of our minds" (Romans 12:2). According to this scripture, renewal of the mind results in the transformation of a person.

If you want to change someone, you just need to renew their minds or change their way of thinking. The people of the world call this indoctrination or brainwashing.

This explains why we have many "worldly" or "carnal believers." Though their spirits were renewed when they were converted, they still need to renew their minds with the word of God so that an actual transformation can be seen in what they do and say.

If the Word of God is not seriously taught in a church and if believers are not encouraged to study the Word of God, they will remain what the Bible calls baby or carnal Christians. That is people who seem not to be changed on the outside even though they are "new creations" on the inside.

Jesus also said in the book of Mark chapter 7 verse 15 that what defiles a man comes from within not without. He was actually implying that it's the thoughts of a person that have the power to defile a man or even the power to make him good.

Thoughts usually enter the mind of a person through the senses. Later when they are dwelt upon, they move on into the spirit of a person, sometimes called the "heart" by the Bible. This is when they have gained momentum and power and are capable of influencing a person significantly, for better or for worse, if they are not checked.

Many people have different ideas on what can defile a person. In one church where I was the pastor, the members insisted that I not permit ladies who were dressed in pants or trousers in the church and certainly not on the pulpit. I tried in vain to explain to them that it's not ones dressing that can defile that person but their thought life. These people had their own idea of what defiles a person.

It's true that one's thought patterns can influence their dressing habits, but really not vice versa. They are many people who are traditionally dressed in ankle long garb, whose hearts are full of fornication and adultery. The Bible of course tells us to be sensitive to other people because, though our mode of dressing may not defile us, it may do so to others watching us.

This is also true with our diets. What we eat may probably affect our health, but cannot defile us, unless of course we falsely believe that it's doing so—then we can be defiled because the Bible says that "whatsoever is not of faith is sin" (Romans 14:23). Something you eat can only defile you by eating it with condemnation in your heart.

Jesus taught, "There is nothing from without a man, that entering into him can defile him: but the things which come out of him, those are they that defile the man" (Mark 7:15). So defilement originates in our thinking patterns. This is important because many people emphasize trivia instead of the more important things.

Jesus also said that what fills the heart the mouth will speak. He said, "... for of the abundance of the heart his mouth speaketh" (Luke 6:45). All this shows the power of our thought life.

Dominant thoughts will eventually affect what we say and do. When our thoughts eventually end up in the spirit or heart, they start influencing what we say and do.

On the other hand we can say that what one says and does reflects what that person is thinking about. . This is because the spiritual law of thought says that "as man thinketh in his heart so is he" (Proverbs 23:7).

You will eventually start moving toward your dominant thoughts and turn out to be like those thoughts. I say eventually because this may take awhile. Dominant thoughts will eventually start shaping your words and actions and your entire lifestyle.

This is why the Bible warns us to jealously guard our thought life. It tells us to "keep thy heart with all diligence; for out of it are the issues of life" (Proverbs 4:23). Notice here the Bible says it's you who is supposed to guard your thought life, not God. How do we guard our heart or spirit? We do this by keeping out the bad thoughts.

If you don't guard your thought life, wrong thoughts may capture it and start compelling you, sometimes even unconsciously, to say and do wrong things.

This is what happened to King David when he saw Bathsheba, the wife of Uriah, bathing naked. David was not an adulterous person inherently. However, instead of fleeing downstairs or some other place when he saw Bathsheba enter her bathroom with a bathing towel (the Bible advises us to flee fornication), he watched her remove the towel and watched her bath naked until she finished and went out. This poisoned his mind, and soon he was in bed with her and later still ordered the death of her husband.

This clearly shows how powerful thoughts can be. It's up to you to guard your thought life and not to per- mit negative or wrong thoughts to take root in your life because you will have to bear the consequences of these thoughts when they lead you into bondage and later make you say and do wrong things.

We must understand that a battle is raging for our minds—between God and the devil—and whomever we support will end up the winner. God wants to influence you for good using your mind, and the devil wants to influence you for evil still using your mind. God wants to get you thinking by planting wonderful thoughts in your mind. The devil too wants to get you thinking by planting terrible thoughts in your mind. They both know that things start happening once people start thinking.

You need to be careful as to what you permit in your thought life. You need to be careful as to what you read and watch and also to what you listen. People need to be careful about watching pornographic materials.

I was in the USA when they told me how watching pornography over the Internet had ruined many homes. You may think that you are not physically involved when you watch these pictures, but eventually you will be in such bondage that all your life will be affected, and you will even start to be physically involved.

If you are already in such bondage there is hope for you. We are told in the Bible that "the weapons of our warfare are not carnal, but mighty through God to the pulling down of stronghold, casting down imaginations and every high thing that exalteth itself against the knowledge of God, and bringing into captivity every thought to the obedience of Jesus Christ" (2 Corinthians 10:4–5).

We understand from this scripture that sometimes thoughts can become so powerful in our lives that they become what the Bible calls "strongholds." They start exalting themselves against the knowledge of God and his word.

In such instances one needs to fight against these thought using the "weapons of our warfare." The Bible has said that these weapons are able to cast down wrong imaginations and to bring every wrong thought captive to the obedience of Jesus Christ. God has not left us helpless. He has given us weapons we can use against our enemies.

One should first of all start such a fight, by using their will to turn against the negative thoughts. A person cannot be delivered who still cherishes their thoughts. The Bible talks about the importance of our will. It says, "If ye be willing and obedient ye shall eat the good of the land" (Isaiah 1:19). God does not forcefully violate our will. He has left us with the freedom to choose between right and wrong.

The Bible also says in Isaiah chapter 55 verse 7 for the unrighteous man to forsake his thoughts. For God to help, you must be willing to forsake the bad thoughts.

One needs also to fight by renewing his mind with the word of God. I call this the replacement method. You replace the bad thoughts with the good ones, because Jesus taught that when the devil finds the house he left empty, he comes back with seven other demons worse than himself to repossess the house.

One needs to read and study the Bible, attend services where the Word is taught, and also to read, study, and meditate on other Christian literature. These are some of the ways we can renew our minds with the word of God.

The word of God also helps us by enlightening us about the truth. The Bible says that you shall know the truth, and the truth shall set you free—see the book of John chapter 8 verse 32. The Bible says that the word of God is truth in John chapter 17 verse 17.

The Bible calls Satan a liar and the father of lies. The Bible says that he was a liar from the beginning. His holding many people captive through the lies he has deluded them with. You cannot be set free if you keep on holding on a lie.

While preaching in a church in the United States sometime back, I came across a Christian woman who believed her problems were due to a certain "generational curse." This is what she had been told at a certain other church she used to attend, and she had come to believe it. I knew just by looking at her that a demon was oppressing her. I also knew that God could not help her unless she adjusted what she believed. She had to start believing that she was the "blessed of the Lord." She believed more in the curse than the blessing. The Bible says that Jesus has redeemed us from the curse of the law, and it's up to you to believe this.

Over the years as I have been ministering, I have come across people who have been bound for a long time and could not be delivered because they believed in a lie. Such people can only be delivered by teaching them the truth because knowing the truth sets people free.

Praying in the spirit or other tongues also helps a lot in this fight. Praying in the spirit moves us into a spiritual position where we have an advantage over the devil and negative thoughts.

The Bible says to "walk in the spirit" so that we may not fulfill the lusts of the flesh see the book of Galatians chapter 5 verse 16. Praying in the spirit helps us to walk in the spirit. Walking in the spirit is walking in a heavenly atmosphere with the Lord very close to you. It can also mean walking in the Word of God because the Word of God is "spirit and is life."

Sometimes one needs also to pray and fast. Jesus while referring to a demon said that this kind cannot be removed without prayer and fasting—see Mark chapter 9 verse 29.

Many years ago when I was still a "babe" in Christ, the devil literary overrun my mind through deception. Thoughts ran through my mind that I could not control, even though I knew they were bad, terrible thoughts. I could only ask God to forgive me because I had really lost control of my mind. I went for prayer but did not receive my deliverance. I had to give up ministry because I was not at all fit to do so. I was only delivered when together with three other friends fasted for this problem for five days. This was a total fast. Even though this problem had lasted for a long time at least for two years, I was so surprised that at the end of this fast I had returned to normal. I was back on the road. I started preaching once again.

When thoughts turn into strongholds, then many times they require prayer and fasting to dislodge them.

Attending an anointed service can also help because the "yoke shall be destroyed because of the anointing" (Isaiah 10:27). When a strong anointing is present, people are delivered from all sorts of bondages including those of bad thoughts.

The Bible says on a certain day "the power of the Lord was present to heal them" (Luke 5:17). So on this particular day many could expect to be healed and delivered by the healing anointing. The healing or the yoke destroying anointing is not in manifestation all the time. When, however, it's manifesting and is put to use, people are healed and delivered. The battle can be intense, but if one is determined he can break loose.

We should always guard our hearts with all diligence, because it's always easier to deny the devil entry than to evict him after he has established himself on the inside. That's why the Bible tells us not to "give place to the devil" (Ephesians 4:27).

The Bible advises us on some things to think about, which are going to influence us in the right way. Philippians chapter 4 verse 8 tells us to think about things that are honest, just, pure, lovely, of good report, and those with virtue and worthy of praise.

We must understand that this spiritual law, that says that a person is going to become like what he or she is thinking, is very important.

God said of the builders of the "tower of Babel" that they would not fail to do whatever they imagined to do—see Genesis chapter 11 verses 6. That's why he confused their language to weaken their resolve.

A thief cannot go out to steal, unless he has been thinking about stealing for some time. When someone comes and tells you, "I love you, I want to marry you," you can tell that person has been thinking about you for some time, just figuring out when to tell you. Thoughts, whether we know it or not, will eventually affect what we say, do, and become.

Law of Confession

The second spiritual law I would like to look at says that a person shall have what he or she is saying.

In the Bible Jesus says, "... whosoever shall say unto this mountain, be thou removed, and be thou cast into the sea; and shall not doubt in his heart, but shall believe that those things which he saith shall come to pass; he shall have whatsoever he saith" (Mark 11:23).

In the above scriptures, the Bible mentions the word *say* three times, underlining its importance. You can have what you say if you keep on saying it. When you keep saying something you keep hearing it, and you will start believing it because "faith cometh by hearing" (Romans 10:17). Even if at the onset you never believed in something, if you keep on hearing it, it starts creating faith in your heart. So what you keep on saying, you keep on hearing, and what you keep on hearing you will eventually believe.

Kenneth Hagin testifies how his wife was sick, and she repeatedly heard the "healing scriptures" tape. She found herself healed. As she kept on hearing these healing scriptures, she eventually received the faith to be healed. This is what people need to do when they need their healing, that is to keep on, again and again, listening to the "healing scriptures" or sermons.

Jesus also says in the Bible that by our words we shall be justified, and by our words we shall be condemned—see Matthew chapter 12 verse 37. Whether we know it or not, God uses our words or what we are saying to reward us. It's a yardstick God uses to judge us. For example you will not be able on judgment day to claim that you got saved if you never confessed Jesus as Lord and Savior. You will not claim that you believed in the heart Jesus to be your Lord and Savior. Nobody will believe you. That's not good enough unless of course you were dumb and could not speak.

On the other hand, the devil also monitors what you are saying to accuse you before God. What you are saying is some of the evidence he is using against you. The Bible calls the devil the accuser of the brethren who is accusing them before our God day and night—see Revelation chapter 12 verse 10.

There is power in what we say or confess, and eventually we shall have whatever we are saying or confessing. Our confession has a way it commits us to something. If you confess doing something, you become more committed to doing that thing than to simply think about doing it.

We read in the Bible that, "a man's belly or stomach shall be satisfied with the fruit of his mouth and with the increase of his lips shall he be filled" (Proverbs 18:20).

So your mouth, or what you are using with it, is capable of feeding you. What you are saying can provide for you financially.

We read in the Bible that "Death and life are in the power of the tongue" and that "they that love it shall eat the fruit thereof" (Proverbs 18:21). This underlines the importance of our words. Our words can kill or give life.

The Bible has said in the above verse of scripture that if we love the tongue we shall eat its fruit. We must appreciate the gift of speaking that God has endowed us with, because this enables us to change our circumstances. We must emphasize speaking but in a positive way. In this way we show love for our tongues and start reaping benefits from it. Some people love the tongue but in a negative way. They speak a lot, but much of what they are saying is foolishness.

What you are saying with your tongue is capable of blessing you or cursing you. It's capable of hindering you or promoting you. It's capable of providing for you or cutting off your supplies.

We read in the Bible that, "thou art snared with the words of your mouth thou art taken with the words of thy mouth" (Proverbs 6:2).

We must be careful about what we are saying lest we hinder ourselves. That why James advises, us in the book he wrote, to be swift to hear but slow to speak. This is because many people just babble words without weighing carefully what they are saying and the impact they are going to create. Some people are their own enemies by what they are saying.

Take for example the man who came to King David to inform him about the death of King Saul on the mountains of Gilboa, in the book of 2 Samuel chapter 1. This man must have been lying because his account of Saul's death differs from the account we read in 1 Samuel chapter 31 verses 4–5. In this account we are told that King Saul fell on his sword and told his armor bearer to finish him off who declined. When the armor bearer saw that he was dead he also killed himself.

The Bible never at all mentions this man who claimed he was the one who had finished Saul off in its own account of Saul's death. This man most probably found Saul and his armor bearer dead and knowing that Saul did not get along with David, sought to get David's favor by claiming he was the one who had finished Saul off. Instead, however, he got a death sentence. David commanded one of his men to execute him, and he told him "that thy blood be upon your head for thy mouth hath testified against thee saying I have slain the Lord's anointed" (2 Samuel 1:16). So what killed this man was not what he did but what he said. It was his lying mouth that slew him.

Your mouth is capable of ensnaring you and even killing you, like it did this man. Many people are hindered from going forward, because of the negative things they keep on saying.

Look also at the twelve men who went to spy out the land on behalf of the children of Israel in the book of Numbers chapters 13 and 14. Whereas all of them concurred that the promised land flowed with milk and honey, ten of them declared that the children of Israel were not "able to go up against the people for they are stronger than we" (Numbers 13:31).

They said they were giants in the land and that the land "eateth up the inhabitants thereof" (Numbers 13:32). They also said that they were like "grasshoppers" before these giants. They brought to the children of Israel what the Bible calls an "evil report." In the end they received exactly what they said. All of them perished in the wilderness.

Conversely two of them Joshua and Caleb brought a good report. "Caleb stilled the people before Moses and Said. Let us go up at once and posses it for we are well able to overcome it" (Numbers 13:30). Both Joshua and Caleb said that "the land which we passed through to search it is an exceeding good land. If the Lord delight in us he will bring us into this land which floweth with milk and honey" (Numbers 14:7–8).

They both were able later to enter the promised land triumphantly as they confessed. They also received what they said, as this second spiritual law we are discussing says, "that you shall have what you keep on saying."

Look at the woman with the issue of blood in the Bible. This woman "…said, if I may touch but his clothes, I shall be whole" (Mark 5:28). This woman went ahead and did what she said, and she was healed of a long time sickness. What she said prompted her to act. She got what she said.

Look at David when he went to fight with Goliath. He told Goliath that "…This day will the Lord deliver thee into mine hand; and I will smite thee, and take thine head from thee; and I will give the carcasses of the host of the Philistines this day unto the fowls of the air and to the wild beasts of the earth; that all the earth may know that there is a God in Israel" (1 Samuel 17:46). David that day got what he boldly confessed.

Real faith speaks. It cannot keep silent. The Bible says, "We having the same spirit of faith, according as it is written, I believed, and therefore have I spoken; we also believe, and therefore speak" (2 Corinthians 4:13). We having the same spirit of faith; as whom? As the Fathers in the faith. You see we are not the authors of the faith neither are we the finishers. Faith does not start and finish with us.

Jesus is the author and finisher of our faith. There is also what the Bible calls a "cloud of witnesses" that has gone before us. These people had speaking faith. The Bible tells us some of the things they said.

They said boldly, "the Lord is my helper and I will not fear what man shall do unto me" (Hebrews 13:6).

They said, "The Lord is my Shepherd; I shall not want" (Psalms 23:1).

They said, "The Lord is my light and my salvation; whom shall I fear? The Lord is the strength of my life; of whom shall I be afraid?" (Psalms 27:1)

They said, "I shall not die but live and declare the works of the Lord" (Psalms 118:17).

Has it ever occurred to you that these saints made these positive confessions when they were facing adverse circumstances? They were using these confessions to fight the adverse circumstances. The fathers in the faith or the cloud of witnesses made positive confessions in the face of life's challenges. What are you saying yourself in the face of these adverse circumstances?

For us to get the same results they got we must have the same "spirit of speaking faith." Our faith has to speak, like theirs did, and as it does, it will bring into reality those things we are believing God for. If our faith does not speak we shall not be able to get the same results they got.

What we are saying, I must stress, has to be positive or what the Bible calls a good report. Faith always has a good report. Some people are speaking all right, but there is a lot of negativity in what they are saying.

God himself seems to operate by this law. In Mark chapter 11 verse 22 Jesus told his disciples to have faith in God. In some Bibles this is rendered in the margins or footnotes to mean or to refer to the "God Kind of faith." This means that Jesus was telling his disciples to have the "God kind of faith." This indicates that God also operates by faith. Jesus had just used this God kind of faith to curse a fig tree. He just spoke to it, and it started drying from the roots. He was advising the disciples to also use this type of speaking faith, to move away the mountains in their lives.

God clearly has speaking faith. He did not only speak the world into existence, the Bible says that Abraham believed before God "who calls those things which are not as though they were" (Romans 4:17). God calls those things which are not as though they are, and as he does this they turn into realty.

How did Abraham know that God does this? He knew because God changed his name and that of his wife Sarah. His name was originally Abram, which means, "exalted father," but God started calling him Abraham, which means, "father of many nations." God was confessing by this that Abraham was the father of many nations even though at the time he was apparently childless and his wife barren. God used the new name to chase away barrenness from Abraham's home.

So do you want to overcome life's challenges? Then learn from God. Start calling those things that are not as though they are. Some people are good at "calling" those things that are as though they are, but they don't know this secret of "calling" those things that are not as though they are; that's why they can't speak these things into existence the way God does. What I mean is that many people "call" or base their confessions on the way things appear at the moment not on the way they want those things to appear. For instance, Jesus said that Jairus's daughter was sleeping but most people would say she was dead. He was not looking at this situation the way it appeared on the surface but was making a confession of faith in God. According to his faith, death was like sleep.

Many times we are defeated because we keep saying what our senses are telling us instead of what God is saying in his Word, which may be saying something entirely different. We should always side with God's Word even in the face of contradicting circumstances. The Bible calls

Gods Word "the truth." This may sometimes be different from the facts. As we side with the truth of God's word, it will cause the facts to line up with it.

Some people think they are being honest by always speaking out what they see and hear and how they feel. This may sometimes, however, be a hindrance to them. It may hinder their faith. It's always profitable to confess the truth of God's Word in a situation instead of the facts. This is not a denial of the facts but an emphasis of what's helpful.

This is why the Bible encourages us to hold fast our profession or confession of faith without wavering, see the book of Hebrews chapter 10 verse 23. This is because as we do so, we are causing what we are confessing to come to pass.

Law of Attraction

The next spiritual law I want to discuss is called the law of attraction, and this law says that you can only attract what you respect. This law says that whatever you desire in life that you don't have, you can attract if you show it total respect.

It can be an anointing or someone or an education. Whatever you respect, you start picking up interest in and start attracting.

Even a baby can tell someone who respects it. When the baby enters a room, he or she will bypass many people and go to their mother who respects them. Even a dog can tell someone who respects it and will move toward that person.

Look at the way Elisha received a double portion of the anointing that was upon Elijah. When Elijah was passing by and threw his mantle on Elisha to signify God's call upon his life, Elisha was quick to give up his job (he was a farmer), and follow Elijah. He even killed the oxen he was using to plow his land, cooked it (using the wood that made up the yoke), and served it to the people on his village. This showed a total consecration and respect to this call. There was no turning back for him.

Look at the way he served Elijah faithfully in the menial position of a servant, right up to the end of Elijah's life and ministry. Look at the way he followed Elijah up to the very end. The Bible tells us that both Elijah and the sons of the prophets tried to discourage him from following Elijah to the end. Elijah probably was testing his commitment. But Elisha insisted on following him to the very end.

The sons of the prophets tried to chide him about this, but he told them to hold their peace and that he knew exactly what he was doing.

Near the end Elijah told him to ask whatever he wanted. That's when he asked for a double portion of the anointing that was upon the life of Elijah. Elijah said that was a hard thing but Elisha managed to get this anointing because he showed it maximum respect and interest.

The sons of the prophets, however, were not able to get this anointing, because they never showed any respect for it. Watching from afar, however, they could tell that Elisha had received it because he was also able to divide the river Jordan like Elijah did. They then came and bowed themselves before Elisha.

The Bible says in Mark chapter 3 verse 14 that Jesus ordained twelve that they should be with him and that he might send them forth to preach. Notice here that the Bible says that Jesus ordained twelve disciples, later called the apostles to first of all be with him. The reason why he wanted to stay with them for some time was so that he could impart to them a "spiritual gift" because you can only impart such a gift through association.

To attract something you must respect it and be willing to spend quality time with that thing or that someone.

The reason why some anointing dies when an anointed person dies is that many people are not willing to pay the price of association to get this anointing.

Many people just want to "take" the anointing as they say. They want to get the anointing on a "silver plate" as it were. This is, however, far from the truth. You can only get one's anointing by spending time or associating with that person. You must sit at his feet and listen to his sermons for some good amount of time. You can only get it by reading many of that person's books and hearing many of his or her compact discs, digital video recordings, etc.

It's also the reason why some people find problems in dating and finding Mister or Miss Right. Some people, young men especially, just want to propose marriage to a beautiful sister without taking time to build a relationship. That's why they are turned down most of the time because they don't obey the law of attraction. Many of them end up with broken hearts.

However much you are anointed, you may not be able to minister on a certain platform simply because you are not associated with the owners of that platform.

We must also be careful about whom we often hang out with or who our friends are. The Bible says, "he that walketh with wise men shall be wise but a companion of fools shall be destroyed" (Proverbs 13:20).

The spirit of the people you often hang out with shall eventually be transferred to you and vice versa. If they are wise, their wisdom will eventually start rubbing off on you. That's why you don't want to hang out with fools lest you get their foolish spirit and be destroyed together with them.

They are some people the Bible refuses us to associate with lest we attract their bad character. The Bible tells us, "Make no friendship with an angry man; and with a furious man thou shalt not go; lest thou learn his ways, and get a snare to thy soul" (Proverbs 22:24–25).

On the other hand they are people the Bible encourages us to hang out with. The Bible tell us that after the disciples were persecuted in Acts chapter 4 verse 23 they went to their own company, and reported all that the chief priests and elders had said unto them. We read later on in that meeting, that they conducted prayers for these problems, which God answered mightily. Your own company, or people the Bible calls of "like precious faith," are people you need to hang out with.

Watch out who your friends are. It's safe to love some people from a distance. Don't let everyone into your inner circle of friends. Some people have done this to their own hurt.

The Bible says, "Evil company corrupt good manners" (1 Corinthians 15:33).

This is also the reason why the Bible tells us:

> Be ye not unequally yoked together with unbelievers; for what fellowship hath righteousness with

unrighteousness? And what communion has light with darkness and what concord has Christ with Belial? Or what part has he that believeth with an infidel? And what agreement hath the temple of God with idols?

For ye are the temple of the living God; as God has said I will dwell in them, and walk in them and I shall be their God and they shall be my people.

Wherefore come out from among them and be ye separate saith the Lord and touch not the unclean thing and I will receive you and will be a Father unto you and ye shall be my sons and daughters saith the Lord Almighty

2 Corinthians 6:14–18

Here the Bible warns us against associating deeply with unbelievers. Of course, we cannot avoid them altogether, but we must be careful how far we go, because "transference of spirits" is very real.

Be careful about joining deeply in business or any other venture with nonbelievers, because you may be dragged into malpractices by them.

The Bible discourages us getting married to nonbelievers for the new couples. Because marriage is a very close bond that the devil can easily use to force the believer to compromise.

In the Bible, the Apostle Paul writes that the widow is at "liberty to be married to whom she will; only in the Lord" (1 Corinthians 7:39). Many people, desperate to get married, have refused to heed this admonition and have had to endure miserable lives that are full of compromise, because marriage is not something you can move in and out of as you wish. Once you are done, you are supposed to stay with it, at least according to God. Others are sometimes forced to go through the process of divorce, with all the accompanying trauma and condemnation. They could have avoided this altogether by taking heed to the word of God in the first place.

The law of attraction is very important to learn because it helps you attract those good things you want to attract in life. It also helps you avoid attracting those bad things you would not wish to attract inadvertently. Whatever good thing you don't have, but you want to attract, you can do so if you show that thing maximum respect and interest.

You can attract money by showing it some respect. Associate with people who have made money, and learn from them how they made it. Be willing to learn from the Holy Spirit or through the teachers he sends you on how to multiply money in your life.

Be generous with what God has given you. Give your tithes, learn to work hard, and be wise on how you invest and spend.

Avoid borrowing unless it's absolutely necessary. You can learn all these things by associating with certain ministries that teach them. Slowly but surely you will start attracting money in your life.

Money just doesn't come in one's life by chance unless they inherit it or win a lottery draw. People get money by actively attracting it in their lives.

Law of Recognition

The fourth law I would like to discuss is the law of recognition. This law basically says that whatever you do not recognize, will eventually exit your life.

God may place certain things and people in your life in order to bless you, but if you do not recognize them, they will leave your life after sometime. These people or things may not be your preferred choice, but you still have to recognize and appreciate them.

In the book of Luke chapter 19 verses 41–44 Jesus wept for the city of Jerusalem because they failed to recognize the time of their visitation.

This city was expecting Jesus to visit them for a long time, actually for many years, but when he did come, they did not recognize him and rejected him.

John says in chapter 1 verse 10 of his book that Jesus was in the world and the world was made by him and the world knew him not. In the next verse he says Jesus, " ... came to his own and his own received him not. But as many as received him to them gave him power to become the sons of God even to them that believe on his name" (John 1:11).

According to this scripture, many of the children of Israel, who were supposed to be the first to become the sons of God, did not do so because they did not receive Jesus. They did not recognize him for whom he was and so missed out.

Whatever God gives you, if you don't recognize it for whatever reason it will eventually exit your life.

In the Bible God says:

> All those men which have seen my Glory and my miracles which I did in Egypt and in the wilderness and have tempted me now these ten times and have not hearkened to my voice surely they shall not see the land which I swore unto their fathers neither shall any of them that provoked me see it.
>
> Numbers 14:22–23

God performed mighty miracles in Egypt in order to free the children of Israel from bondage. These miracles were also to help the children of Israel recognize who God was. With this recognition they would have behaved in a certain way when facing the challenges in the wilderness. Unfortunately most of them failed to recognize him and so perished in the wilderness.

In the book of Mathew chapter 16 verses 15–17 Jesus asks his disciples who the people were saying he was. He was wondering whether the many people who followed him, recognized who he really was. According to the response of his disciples, most of Jesus's many followers really did not recognize who he really was.

Peter, with the help of the heavenly Father, was able to get a revelation of who Jesus really was, and Jesus says because of that he was blessed. A person is really blessed if he or she can understand who God really is, and what he's doing in his or her life.

Jesus, also in the book of Mark chapter 8 verses 17–21, rebukes his disciples for failing to recognize him and what he was capable of doing, even after witnessing more than one multiplication miracle of bread and fish to feed the hungry multitudes. This is because these disciples thought that Jesus was worried about what they would eat when he told them to "beware the leaven of the Pharisees and the leaven of Herod" (Mark 8:15). He asks them, "Having eyes see ye not? And having ears hear ye not? And do ye not remember?" (Mark 8:18).

The miracles God is doing in our lives are supposed to help us recognize him as El Shadai or the God who is more than enough. This would enable us be bold in our faith when we are confronted with other challenges in life.

I like what Paul the apostle says in the Bible. After testifying on how God delivered them from "so great a death" (2 Corinthians 1:10), he goes on to say that the same God was presently delivering them and also declared boldly his expectation of Gods deliverance in the future.

Failure to recognize God and what he is doing in our lives can be costly because this spiritual law says that whatever we do not recognize shall eventually exit our lives. There are many people who are living a life of regret, having realized later the great opportunities that God had availed them that they had not used.

I am sure that the people who find themselves in hell live this life of regret forever. I read of a certain young man who stood up to go to the altar to give his life to the Lord when they gave the altar call, but later changed his mind because his fellow young men made fun of him. Even before this service was over, they all left in a car laughing and were run over by a train, whose tracks ran behind this church. All of these young men died. I believe that this young man is living a life of regret forever because he never utilized this last opportunity that God had given him to give his life to Jesus.

One lady wished to restore her marriage because she concluded her former husband had not been so bad after all, but it was too late. Her former husband had moved on with his life.

If you don't want to live a life of regret, always be someone who has "eyes to see" and "ears to hear" what God is doing in your life.

You need to recognize the voice of the Holy Spirit. Jesus said his people are supposed to know his voice—see John chapter 10 verse 4. The Bible also says, "... as many as are led by the Spirit of God they are the Sons of God" (Romans 8:14).

Elijah recognized the voice of the Holy Spirit. The Bible says in 1 Kings chapter 19 verses 11–13 that as he was standing before the Lord on the mountain there was a wind, but he could tell that the Lord was not in the wind.

Then there was the earthquake and he could tell that God was not in the earthquake.

Then there was the fire but God was not in the fire.

Then there was a small, still voice, and he could tell that was God. When he heard it he wrapped his face in his mantle. This contradicts many people's belief that God always manifests in a noisy or loud environment.

The voice of God will lead you in paths of blessing, protection, joy, and peace if you recognize it; and if you miss it you will forfeit these things.

How does the Holy Spirit lead us or speak to us? One way he does this, is through the written Word of God. The Bible says that holy men spoke and wrote the Bible as they were moved by the Holy Spirit—see 2 Peter 1 verse 21. So when you find yourself at a crossroad, always first consider what the *logos* or the written word says about that subject.

For example the Holy Spirit will always lead you in the way of love because God is love. So the Holy Spirit most likely is not the one leading you to start a church next door to another one because this may gender strife.

He will certainly not be the one leading you to directly persuade sheep from another congregation to join yours because this is tantamount to stealing sheep.

The Holy Spirit also leads us by the inward intuition or witness. The Bible says that the Holy Spirit convicts men of sin righteousness and judgment. This conviction takes place in the hearts of men.

In the book of Romans chapter 8 verse16, the Bible says that the Holy Spirit witnesses with our spirits that we are the sons of God. So one way we can tell that we are the children of God is by the inward witness.

Paul, in the book of Romans chapter 9 verse 1, says he had a witness in the Holy Spirit that he preferred to be accursed or to be locked out of heaven for the sake of his fellow Jews. What a loving man!

You need to follow your heart and the convictions or witnesses, placed there by the Holy Spirit. Don't ignore these convictions. When you sense a red light or hindrances in your spirit, don't go through with whatever you are going to do. When you sense a green light go ahead, the Lord is with you.

If you have no peace of mind, don't go ahead with whatever you want to do. The Bible says we should let the peace of God rule in our hearts and minds—see Colossians 3 verse 15. Having peace of mind about something is a good indication that the Lord is with you.

Do always examine those strong desires and impressions that come in your spirit. A lack of strength and energy to do something many times shows that you are doing something in the flesh and not in the spirit. Whenever the Holy Spirit leads you to do something he will energize you to do it.

Many people are living a life of regret and loss because they ignored the inward witness. Paul, while being taken as a prisoner to Rome, admonished his fellow travelers and said, " ... Sirs, I perceive that this voyage will be with hurt and much damage, not only of the lading and ship but also of our lives" (Acts 27:10). Nobody, however, believed him. Later when they hit a terrible storm he stood up and told them, "Sirs, you should have hearkened to me not to have loosed from Crete and to have gained this harm and loss" (Acts 27:21).

A widow of a certain young pastor, who perished in a plane accident as he traveled to preach one Sunday morning, testified how that very morning her husband woke up quite early and told her he sensed he should not go on that trip. But nevertheless he ignored that witness and went.

Many people were wondering why a young pastor with a young wife, baby kids, and a thriving church should be taken to heaven at that time. This provided the answer. It was not the will of God for this pastor to die at that time. He actually tried to warn him not to go, but he did not heed the warning.

One day I felt strongly led to visit a certain family. When I was leaving they handed me five hundred U.S. dollars. Another time I felt impressed to call someone. He asked me to come and see him. As soon as I arrived he got some money unexpectedly. He gave me a good amount of that money.

This conviction is stronger when a lot to lose is at stake. If it's a matter of life and death, then this conviction will be more authoritative.

You can also stay under this conviction for some time. In one instance I had a strong conviction for about a month and half telling me to read my Bible. I was still a baby Christian and I was about to sit my final exams at the university. Every student was busy revising their notes in preparation for these exams, and this seemed the logical thing to do, but because the witness seemed to be so urgent, I read my Bible instead. I later understood why when sooner than later I met a very severe trial. God used the scriptures I had stored in my spirit at that time to sustain me.

The Holy Spirit sometimes leads us by speaking to us in an audible voice. Here it's not just a feeling, but the Holy Spirit forms actual words in a specific language (He knows all languages). This we must emphasize is not an everyday phenomenon.

If you read the book of Acts you will find that several times the Holy Spirit spoke to the disciples in an audible voice. He spoke to Peter after he had seen the vision of the "sheet" to go with the men who had come to fetch him "doubting nothing" (Acts 10:20) because he had sent them.

He spoke to Stephen and told him to join himself to the chariot of the Ethiopian eunuch.

He spoke to the ministers who were ministering to the Lord with fasting in the Bible and instructed them to "separate me Barnabas and Paul for the work whereunto I have called them" (Acts 13:1–20).

One time I was facing a big challenge and did not know where to turn. I was talking with my mother, who was suggesting that I go to some church she knew some place, when all of a sudden the Holy Spirit spoke in my local dialect in an audible voice and told me to "go to

Kayiwa's place." Kayiwa is the name of the senior pastor of that church.

I obeyed this voice and left that evening for Kayiwa's place, and that's where I got my deliverance. In fact I thought I was to go there only for that evening, but it turned into years. I joined that church and became a minister there. That's where I got married to my wife.

I must emphasize that the Holy Spirit speaks to us audibly when it's absolutely necessary. This is when sometimes you are facing very important choices in life with far-reaching repercussions. The Holy Spirit doesn't speak to us lightly this way. He also does it by his own initiative.

We should pray for him to communicate to us, but it may not necessarily be in an audible voice. He has other ways as we are seeing of communicating to us. I say this because the Bible says they are many voices in this world and none of them without significance. We should be open to whatever method he chooses to use. We should be careful not to insist on an audible voice because you don't want the devil to take advantage of you.

Another way the Holy Spirit leads us is through angels. Angels are heavenly beings that can sometimes appear to men as God wills. Though you can sense the presence of angels when they are leading you, God will enable you to see them and hear what they have to say using the gift of "discernment of spirits." The Bible calls angels ministering spirits sent to minister to the heirs of salvation—see Hebrews 1 verse 14.

In the book of Acts we see an angel telling Cornelius to call for Peter who was going to tell him words by which he would be saved—see Acts Chapter 10 verse 5–7.

Also in the book of Acts chapter 8 verse 20, an angel tells Philip to go toward the south on the road from Jerusalem to Gaza which is desert. There Philip met and evangelized the Ethiopian eunuch.

In the book of Acts, the apostles had been locked up in the common prison, but an angel of the Lord released them and commanded them to continue preaching all the "words of this life" (Acts 5:19–20). So God can use angels to direct you.

You must however judge all the visions you see, because the Bible says that sometimes the devil transforms himself into an "angel of light," while trying to deceive people—see 2 Corinthians chapter 11 verse 14. All visions of angels and any other vision must line up with the word of God.

Apart from angels, the Lord leads us through visions and dreams, and we also see this in the book of Acts. Peter, while praying, saw a vision in which the Lord was directing him to evangelize the Gentiles. Before that he and the church evangelized only the Jews—see Acts chapter 10 verses 10- 16.

Notice that the Bible says Peter did not understand this vision right away. Visions and dreams sometimes need interpretation and cannot just be interpreted literary. In the book of Acts chapter 9, the Apostle Paul saw two visions, in which the Lord Jesus directed him to do certain things.

As I pointed out earlier, not all visions are of the Lord, and you have to judge them. They are different types of visions. They are what are called spiritual visions that you see when your eyes are closed. This type of vision is the one Paul saw when the Lord was directing him to Ananias's place, because he had already been blinded by the bright light of the glory of the Lord.

Then there are visions you see when you fall into a trance. Here your senses are sort of temporarily suspended.

Then there are open visions that you see when your senses are intact.

God also leads us through dreams, which are visions we see when we are sleeping. The Bible says in the book of Acts chapter 16 verse 9, that a vision appeared to Paul in the night. I believe Paul saw a dream while sleeping at night.

Another way the Holy Spirit may lead us is through the prophets. In the book of Acts chapter 21 a certain prophet by the name of Agabus bound himself with Paul's girdle and warned him of imprisonment at Jerusalem. This was actually not an instruction on what to do. It was just a forecast of what was going to happen, and it was Paul's call whether to go or not.

In the book of Acts chapter 13 verse 2, Paul and Barnabas received a prophetic word to begin their apostolic ministry. Many other times in the Bible prophets gave to people words of guidance.

Prophets in the New Testament, however, minister differently from the ones in the Old Testament. They mainly come, to confirm what one has already received from the Lord, the reason being that all of the believers now have the Spirit of the Lord—see 1 Corinthians chapter 7 verse 40. Here Paul reminded the believers that he also had the Spirit of God and was, therefore, also capable of making the right judgment.

In the Old Testament, the Holy Spirit was the exclusive reserve of a few people, namely the king, prophet, and the priest. To inquire of the Lord, one had to go to these people.

God promised in the New Testament to pour his Spirit upon all flesh. I believe here the Lord was referring to born-again people. So now everyone can directly approach God and also directly receive an answer from him because we all have the Holy Spirit.

People need to be careful about personal prophesies, because if they are not really from the Lord, they can lead people into error and can cause divisions and confusion. Don't just run with any prophesy that you don't have a witness for in your spirit. If it's for the future, the witness may not be there yet, so you just need to keep the prophecy and wait for the witness to come.

The Bible tells us to judge prophesies and really confirm whether they are from the Lord. We are told in the book of 1 Thessalonians to "despise not prophesying but to prove all things" (1 Thessalonians 5:20).

We are also told in the book of 1 Corinthians to "let the prophets speak two or three and to let the other judge" (1 Corinthians 14:20). All prophesies need to be judged. We should not shut off the gift of prophesy but examine whether it's being used correctly.

You must realize that the Lord eventually holds you responsible for whatever you choose to believe and whatever voice you choose to follow. You cannot claim you were deceived, because you have the written word of God and the Spirit of truth dwelling on the inside of you.

We need to judge all prophesies by the Word of God and by the witness we have in our spirits.

We need also to consider the doctrine sometimes. Does it agree with some of the major tenets of our faith? I say major because they may be some minor things we may disagree that leave the principal tenets intact.

We need to judge certain prophesies on whether they come to pass or not—see the book of Deuteronomy chapter 18 verse 22. If what was said does not come to pass, then we know that was not the Lord. They are, however, some conditional prophesies (prophesies that will come to pass only after certain conditions are met), and we need to distinguish these.

If someone on a continuous basis prophesies things that don't come to pass, we may be forced to write her or him off as a Prophet of God, even though this may hurt their feelings. They clearly may not have what it takes for this office.

We need to judge prophesies on whether they glorify the Lord Jesus or just a mere man. The Bible says the Holy Spirit is there to glorify Jesus.

We need to judge prophesies on whether they are leading people into bondage or they are liberating people. Be careful about so-called prophets who try to enslave you using a spirit of fear. The Bible says that God has not given us a spirit of fear but of power, love, and sound mind. It's okay sometimes to remind people that our God is "a consuming fire," but this is different from some people who try to make others afraid of them. As I said earlier the Holy Spirit is there to glorify Jesus not to promote men's egos.

We need also to judge prophesies by considering the character of the prophet because the Bible says that we shall be able to tell false prophets by the fruit they are bearing in their lives. All human beings have weaknesses, but some people's character shows that they are not even born again in the first place.

Lastly, God may lead us through counsel from other people, and even sometimes through outward circumstances, but this is not a very reliable way; and we must insist on having a witness in our spirits, since they have been recreated at the new birth.

Things may not be going well or as you planned, but this does not necessarily mean that you are outside the will of God. Jesus told his disciples to go to the other side of the lake, yet on the way there they encountered a storm. If things are not working out, sometimes you need to start inquiring of the Lord to make sure you are on the right track.

Sometimes when things are not going on well for a considerable amount of time, God may be getting your attention to move on. When Jacob was staying with his uncle Laban and had started prospering, he started facing antagonism from Laban and his sons, and the Lord told him it was now time to go back home.

It's very important to learn to recognize the voice of the Holy Spirit and his leadings.

Also concerning the Holy Spirit, you need to recognize when he is moving or when the anointing is in manifestation so that you can strike the "iron when it's still hot." God always anoints us for a purpose, and we need to recognize this purpose and use the anointing for it.

The anointing of God doesn't come upon us to simply enjoy, though it's always pleasurable to be in a strong presence of God. This is why Peter did not want to leave the mountain of transfiguration but wanted to build three tents—one for Jesus one for Moses and one for Elijah. This is also why people don't want to leave, a heavily anointed service at the end.

Even though the anointing is pleasurable, God anoints us with more in mind than simply us feeling great. He wants to use the anointing to help people in need. He wants us to use the anointing to draw people to the altar to be saved, to heal and deliver people.

We need to understand the importance of timing. Some people don't use the anointing when it's in manifestation and come for prayers after it has lifted. This is mistiming.

When the anointing is in manifestation or present, that's when it's the right time to minister healing and deliverance. If the anointing is not used to help people who need it or if it's just used to dance and shout, it's in a sense wasted. Dancing and shouting is supposed to be a bonus not the main thing. It has its place, but we should not substitute it for what really God wants to achieve with the anointing.

Secondly you need to recognize the call of God upon your life or your assignment in this life. Your blessings and satisfaction in life are interwoven closely with your assignment. You will never be satisfied in life unless you are in the middle of God's call upon your life. This is the reason why we have many Christians living dissatisfied lives.

The Bible tells us not to be unwise but to know what the will of God is for our life, because herein lies our blessings, satisfaction, and peace. Being outside of the will of God is a sign that one lacks wisdom and is also a mark of foolishness, which is the opposite of wisdom. We cannot excel in life if we are just doing anything that comes our way instead of concentrating on what God has called us to do.

One good indication of your assignment is something that you have a burden for and delight in doing. It's up to you to discover whatever God has called you to do so that you may live a fruitful and rewarding life.

Proverbs says, "It is the glory of God to conceal a thing but the honor of Kings is to search out a matter" (Proverbs 25:2). It's your honor to search and find out God's will for your life. You need to recognize the gifts the Lord has endowed you with so that you may "stir them up." The Bible says that we have differing gifts. It also says that "a man's gift makes room for him and bringeth him before great men" (Proverbs 18:16). Realizing your gift and concentrating on it can result in you becoming great or renown with an increase in your paycheck.

You need also to recognize the people God has placed in your life to help you fulfill whatever he has called you to do. You cannot fulfill what God has called you to do alone. You need the help of God and the help of people God will assign to you.

In the Bible, we have what is called the "ministry of helps," and I believe this is a very important ministry—see 1 Corinthians chapter 12 verse 28. God, in the book of Isaiah, says that he is going to help us—see chapter 44 verse 2.

When David was in the "hold" hiding from King Saul, God sent people to help him. We read in 1 Chronicles that when some of these people came to him, the Spirit of the Lord came upon Amasai, and he prophesied saying, "Thine are we David and thy side thou son of Jesse peace be unto thee and peace be to thine helpers for thy God helpeth thee" (1 Chronicles 12:18). This was because David was querying these people to see whether they were for him or whether they had come to betray him to King Saul. He was ascertaining who they really were, in effect recognizing them.

You need to recognize these God sent helpers and celebrate them and choose on purpose not to antagonize them. Elijah recognized that God had commanded the widow of Zarephath to sustain him during the terrible famine—see 1 Kings Chapter 17 verse 9.

Not everybody has been assigned by God to help you. Some people will not at all be concerned about your problem. You need to discover the people God has assigned to help you. They are some people out there whom God wants to use to bless you financially.

Had Elijah not gone to Sidon, to the widow of Zarephath, he would have got no help. Many people are looking for help in all the wrong places. That's why they are disappointed and heartbroken all the time.

You need to find the right people to help you and to concentrate on them. You need to appreciate and "handle them with care" as they say; because if you lose them they can leave a void that nobody may be able to fill for some time. Treat them respectfully and avoid arrogant behavior toward them because you cannot afford to lose them. Always be thankful for them and pray for them. You need to recognize the doors of favor God has opened for you and to concentrate on these doors instead of trying to breakdown closed doors.

The devil also is aware of these people and will do his best to spoil your relationship with these people, to deny you the help they are giving you, so be on the watch.

Another thing you need to recognize are your enemies. All nations around the world operate spy organizations because they want to recognize their enemies. The Bible says that we should not be "ignorant of the devil's devices"—see 2 Corinthians chapter 2 verse 11. In that same verse the Bible says that if we are ignorant of the devil's devices, he will eventually get an advantage over us. So we need to recognize our enemies.

Jesus was well aware of his enemies who were trying to catch him in his words, so he answered them wisely and left them baffled. He was well aware that the devil was after Peter and had asked God to sift him like wheat so he prayed for Peter. In contrast Peter did not know what the devil was up to, so he fell into temptation. Had Jesus not prayed for him, Peter would have fallen for good.

David recognized that Saul was envious of him, so he behaved himself wisely. He did not want to make the situation worse. That's why he survived him.

Jesus recognized that the devil was using Peter to discourage him from going to the cross so he told him "to get behind me, Satan."

Jesus recognized that the devil was twisting scriptures when he told him to jump from the highest point of the Temple, because God said he was going to give "angels charge over him so that he does not dash his feet against a stone."

Paul, in Acts chapter 16, recognized that the young girl who went about advertising them had a spirit of divination, so he cast it out. Even though what the girl was actually saying was true (they were servants of the most high God showing people the way of salvation), yet who wants the devil to advertise him any way? Whenever the devil advertises you like this way, he is up to some mischief.

If you don't recognize your enemy, that enemy will defeat you. Samson refused to recognize Delilah as an enemy instead of simply a "lover girl," and he was defeated.

Recognizing an enemy will help you guard against that enemy and avoid being defeated. They are mainly two sides to an enemy. God permits enemies to prove you and promote you, but the devil wants to use those same enemies to defeat you. Joseph told his brothers in Genesis chapter 50 verse 20, that what they had meant for evil God meant for good to save many people from hunger.

You need together with the enemy to recognize your most dominant weakness and deal with it. In Hebrews, we are told to lay aside "the sin which doth so easily beset us" (Hebrews 12:1).

They are areas of weakness we need to recognize and deal with. The Bible says that if we judge ourselves God would not judge us—see 1 Corinthians chapter 11 verse 31.

Clearly King Solomon seemed to have had a weakness for women, for how can one marry a thousand of them? Even though he was the wisest man on the earth, he failed to apply the abundant wisdom he had on this issue.

Recognize your area of weakness, and work on it; otherwise it can turn around and defeat you. King Saul had an ego problem. He, unlike Solomon, did not marry many women but could not stand anyone being more popular than him.

Next you need to recognize men and women of God, especially those God has appointed to raise you up spiritually.

We read in the book of Numbers chapter 16 how Korah connived with 250 of the leaders to oppose the leadership of Moses and Aaron saying they were "taking too much upon themselves." The Bible says that the earth opened up and swallowed them alive. God vindicated Moses and Aaron when he later caused Aaron's rod to bud in Numbers chapter 17.

Korah and his colleagues perished because they failed to recognize the leaders God had placed over them and instead tried to usurp their authority.

Many other people later have followed suit. Many believers over the years have risen up against their spiritual leaders to their own hurt and peril.

Hebrews tells us to "obey them that have the rule over you and submit yourselves for they watch for your souls as they must give account that they may do it with joy and not with grief for that is unprofitable to you" (Hebrews 13:17).

In verse 7 of the same chapter the Bible tells us to "remember them which have the rule over you who have spoken unto you the word of God whose faith follow considering the end of their conversation" (Hebrews 13:7).

If you don't recognize the people God has placed over your spiritual life, he cannot use these people to bless you. When God wants to bless you and develop you spiritually he sends a person into your life, and it's up to you to recognize this person.

Many believers are not well mentored because they refuse to submit to the mentors God sends into their lives.

In the book of 2 Kings, we read the story of this woman who was able to recognize Elisha as a man of God and asked her husband to build him a room where he could rest when he passed their side. She told her husband, "Behold now I perceive that this is a holy man of God which passes by us continually. Let us make a little chamber I pray thee on the wall and let us set for him there a bed and a table and a stool and a candlestick and it shall be when he cometh to us that he shall turn in thither" (2 Kings 4:9–10).

This woman who could not have a child was able to conceive and give birth to a son, and when the devil fought the son and killed him, Elisha raised him from the dead. Other people never received such miracles because they never recognized Elisha for who he was.

Jesus made some interesting but sobering remarks in the book of Luke chapter 4. He said from verse 24, "...verily I say unto you no prophet is accepted in his own country."

He went on to say, "... I tell you of a truth many windows were in Israel in the days of Elijah when the heaven was shut up three years and six months when great famine was throughout all the Land but unto none of them was Elijah sent save unto Sarepta a city of Sidon unto a woman that was a widow" (Luke 4:25).

In verse 27 he says, "and many lepers were in Israel in the time of Elisha the Prophet and none of them was cleansed saving Naaman the Syrian" (Luke 4:27).

Why in God's name would God help foreigners and bypass his people Israel who needed the same help? The answer is simple. The children of Israel failed to recognize and believe the men who God sent them. Even though help was nearby they failed to recognize it, while some people far away did. God says in his Word that his blessings and salvation was to the Jews first, but if they failed to receive them he would turn to the Gentiles.

So you need to recognize the men and women God sends into your life. God has gifted them and anointed them not for themselves but so that you may be blessed, and if you do not recognize the anointing upon their lives, it will not be a blessing to you.

The Bible says that he who welcomes a righteous man in the name of a righteous man shall receive a righteous man's reward and that he who welcomes a prophet in the name of a prophet shall receive a prophet's reward.

Men of God may have personal weaknesses but do recognize the anointing upon their lives. David refused to harm King Saul even when the Spirit of God had departed from him. He composed a song of mourning for him when he died. This clearly shows how much he respected the anointing upon his life.

So recognize men and women of God. They are there to help mature you. In the book of Ephesians chapter 4 we read that God has set in the church first apostles, then prophets, teachers, pastors, and evangelists to equip you and prepare you for the work of the ministry.

You also need to recognize who you are in Jesus Christ. You cannot enjoy the benefits of salvation until you recognize who you became in Christ. You need to recognize that now in Christ you are a new creation or a new creature—see 2 Corinthians chapter 5 verse 17. Your spirit (the real you) was recreated again at the new birth. This means that now you can walk in newness of life. It means that the old life of sin no longer has dominion over you. You old life whatever it was has no longer any power over you.

You need to recognize that in Christ you are now a son or daughter of God. Children resemble their parents in every way, so you need to start resembling your Father God. People should look at you and your conduct and see your Father God because you have his seed in you.

You need also to recognize that in Christ you are the redeemed of the Lord. Jesus has redeemed you from the satanic prison and the devil no longer has authority over you. He has given you "power to tread on serpents and scorpions, and over all the power of the enemy; and nothing shall by any means hurt you" (Luke 10:19). The devil no longer has the power and authority to hurt you in any way if you recognize who you are. You are not supposed to be afraid of him. The devil is the one supposed to run away from you in terror. Sickness also should flee from you in terror.

Unfortunately, many believers today are afraid of the devil and sickness; that's why we see these two still dominating some in the body of Christ. Instead of laughing at sickness many people are paralyzed by fear by it.

You need also to recognize that in Christ you are the blessed of the Lord. The Bible says that God has "blessed us with all spiritual blessings in heavenly places in Christ" (Ephesians 1:3). Money now is supposed to be your friend and poverty is supposed to flee from you.

One may ask: If I have been blessed with all the blessings in heaven why am I still experiencing financial hardships? The answer lies in faith. We get everything God has given us by faith. You need to exercise your faith in this area like Abel did. The Bible says, "... by faith Abel offered unto God a more excellent sacrifice than Cain, by which he obtained witness that he was righteous. God testifying of his gifts: and by it he being dead yet speaketh" (Hebrews 11:4).

Because he had faith in the area of finances, Abel offered a more excellent sacrifice to God than his brother Cain. If you don't have faith in the area of finances, you won't be able to access all these blessings in heaven that God has given you. So let's know who we are in Christ. The Bible says many things about this subject. We have been made kings and priests unto God. We are now Christ ambassadors etc.

Law of Process

"I will not drive them out before thee in one year; lest the land become desolate and the beasts of the field multiply against thee. By little and little I will drive them out from before thee until thou be increased, and inherit the land" (Exodus 24:29–30).

The law of process I believe is very important for us to understand. This law basically says that before God takes you to another level, he will have to pass you through a process.

In the above quoted scriptures, God tells the children of Israel that he would not give them the "promised land" all at once, but they would have to inherit it bit by bit. They would have to go through a process in order to inherit this land.

In this incident, God explains to them why they would have to go through a process. They could not handle the logistics of taking all of it at once. The beasts of the field would multiply against them, and they would not be able to handle them. This was for their good. They were not prepared to take all this land at once. This is one of the reasons why God takes us through a process that is to prepare us to be able to handle the bigger responsibilities.

A person can only handle so much at a certain level of development.

Jesus told the disciples that he could not tell them everything, because they were not able at that time to handle it—see John 16 verse 12.

Paul told the Corinthian believers that he fed them with milk because they were not able at that time to handle strong meat—see 1 Corinthians chapter 3 verse 2.

God passes us through a process, to prepare us for bigger responsibilities and because we can only handle so much at certain times.

The book of Judges says, "...these are the nations which the Lord left to prove Israel by them, even as many of Israel as had not known all the wars of Canaan; Only that the generations of the children of Israel might know, to teach them war, at the least such as before new nothing thereof" (Judges 3:1–2).

Verse 4 says still concerning these nations, "And they were to prove Israel by them, to know whether they would hearken unto the commandments of the Lord, which he commanded their fathers by the hand of Moses" (Judges 3:4).

They were some in the camp of Israel who had not gone through the process, and God catered for them. He purposely left enemies around so that they could learn to fight and so that they could go through the testing process.

Some in the camp had, in a sense, to go through this training a second time for the sake of those who never had an opportunity to train. They had to go through the process a second time for the sake of their children who were born after the initial wars.

Some of the enemies that are still in your life are there to enable you go through the process so that you may be prepared for a greater season.

A child has to pass through a process before he can begin to run. He starts off by being carried by others; then he begins to sit on his own. Later a baby stands up on his two feet without being supported. Then he makes the first steps. He then begins to walk and then later starts to run.

All the men of God in the Bible first passed through a process before they began to minister for him.

The Lord Jesus started ministry when he was about thirty years old, and after being taken by the Holy Spirit into the wilderness to be tempted by the devil, where he fasted for forty days. He could have started his ministry at twenty, but he had to go through the process.

The Bible says that though he was the Son of God, he learnt obedience through the things he suffered. The Bible also says that God made the captain of our "salvation perfect through sufferings" (Hebrews 2:10).

If Jesus had to go through a process to prepare him for the ministry God had called him to do, much more will we have also to go through a process.

David was anointed to be king by Samuel, yet he took several years before he actually became a king; and during this time he was a fugitive running for his life from King Saul.

Moses spent forty years on the backside of the desert looking after sheep that actually did not belong to him. Before he went to the backside of the desert he had killed an Egyptian with his bare hands. However after the forty years period of training, the Bible says he was the meekest man throughout the earth and could not even stand up to his sister, Miriam, and Aaron when they rose up against him in regard to his marriage—see Numbers 12:1–3

In the wilderness or the backside of the desert, that's where we develop character. God in the wilderness teaches us the important lesson of humility. The Bible says that he resists the proud but gives grace to the humble. Also in the wilderness God teaches us patience, love, etc. It's where God instills in us godly character.

God told the children of Israel in the book of Deuteronomy:

> ... thou shall remember all the way which the Lord your God led thee these forty years in the wilderness to humble thee and to prove thee to know what was in your heart whether you would keep his commandments or no.
>
> And he humbled thee and suffered thee to hunger and fed thee with manna which thou knewest not neither did thy fathers know that he might make thee know that man doth not live by bread only but by every word that proceedeth out of the mouth of the Lord doth man live
>
> Deuteronomy 8:2

In these verses of scripture God tells the children of Israel that he led them through the wilderness on purpose to humble them, test them, and also to teach them, not to live by food only but also by the word of God.

The wilderness is a place of training and of testing. It's a place where you sit for your spiritual exams, and if you pass, you are then taken to another level. If, however, you fail, you repeat a test until you pass.

The time you spend in the wilderness can depend upon you. It can depend on how fast you learn and your attitude while there.

The children of Israel spent a very long time in the wilderness—forty years, to be exact—because they were slow learners and because they rebelled against God in the wilderness. They let the wilderness harden them instead of softening them.

We find the warning in 1 Corinthians. It says:

> Moreover brethren I would not that you should be ignorant how that our Fathers were under the cloud and all passed through the sea. And were all baptized unto Moses in the cloud and in the sea. And did all eat the same spiritual meat. And did all drink the same spiritual for they drank of that spiritual Rock that followed them and that Rock was Christ.
>
> But with many of them God was not well pleased for they were overthrown in the wilderness. Now these things were our examples to the intent we should not lust after evil things as they also lusted.

> Neither be ye idolaters as were some of them as it is written the people sat down to eat and drink and rose up to play. Neither let us commit fornication as some of them committed and fell in one day three and twenty thousand. Neither let us tempt Christ as some of them also tempted and were destroyed of serpents. Neither murmur ye as some of them also murmured and were destroyed of the destroyer
>
> 1 Corinthians 10:1–10

The reason why the children of Israel spent such a long time in the wilderness and why many of them perished in the wilderness is because they let evil overcome them there. The wilderness is a place of trials, testing, and pain. It's a place of scarcity and lack. It's a place of humility and reproach. It's a place where the devil loves to take advantage of you because you are vulnerable in many ways.

It's a place where you need to be on your guard. The psalmist asks God to set a watch before his mouth and to keep the door of his lips—see Psalms 141 verse 3. This is very important when you are facing the "day of temptation in the wilderness."

The Bible says of Jesus in the book of Isaiah, "He was oppressed and he was afflicted yet he opened not his mouth: he is brought as a lamb to the slaughter, and as a sheep before her shearers is dumb so he openeth not his mouth" (Isaiah 53:7).

This was the secret of his victory. He refused to commit sin with his mouth when going through the process.

Job refused to "charge God foolishly" even against the advice of his irate wife when going through the trying process—see Job 1 verse 22 and Job 2 verses 9–10. Many people have been defeated by their mouth in the wilderness.

The law of process can either make you or break you. Many people have been defeated in the wilderness because they have not understood the law of process.

Many have wrongly believed that God was penalizing them by the challenges and problems they were facing, instead of understanding that God was preparing them for future seasons.

Many people have become bitter and impatient in the wilderness. The Bible tells us not to allow bitterness to take root in our lives. Jesus said that blessed is the person who does not take offence in him. Others have murmured against God in the wilderness.

As I said the wilderness is a place of suffering. The Bible teaches that there is some good that comes out of suffering. This sometimes may not be evident in the short run but in the long run.

James says to "count it all joy when ye fall into divers temptations knowing this that the trying of your faith worketh patience" (James 1:2–3).

The Apostle Paul says in Romans chapter 5 from verse 3 that he gloried in tribulations because he realized that "tribulations worketh patience and patience experience and experience hope" (Romans 5:3–4).

In 2 Corinthians Paul says, "I take pleasure in infirmities, in reproaches, in necessities, in persecutions, in distresses for Christ's sake for when I am weak then I am strong" (2 Corinthians 12:10).

Jesus says in the book of John, "…except a corn of wheat fall into the ground and die, it abideth alone but if it die it bringeth forth much fruit" (John 12:24). Suffering can make us more Christ-like and more productive in the kingdom of God, if we can endure it.

In the book of Hebrews chapter 12 verse 8, the Bible tells us that all of us are partakers of this "chastisement." There are really no shortcuts. All of us have to go through this process that refines us and makes us "fit for the Master's use." So let us be willing to go through the process.

One of the reasons why there is a lot of sin and crime in the world today is because people don't want to go through the process. People desire the success of other people, but they don't want to go through the process to get this success, so they get it the wrong way. They kill and steal to get success in life instead of laboring for it. There is a godly way to get to the pinnacle of success and that is by going through the process. You don't have to compromise to reach to the top.

Law of Sowing and Reaping

"Be not deceived God is not Mocked: for whatsoever a man soweth that shall he also reap" (Galatians 6:7).

This is probably the most recognized law by the body of Christ, and it says that you shall reap whatsoever you have been sowing.

In the Bible, there are several things that are described as seed. These include, among others, the Word of God, money, plant, seeds, etc. What we sow is what we put in the lives of others. Whether we realize it or not, we are sowing all the time, and the Bible says that one day we are going to reap whatever we have been sowing.

At one point in time what you have been doing to others will be done to you. At one time you will be treated exactly the way you have been treating others. If you have been helping others, at one time you will receive help. If you have been mistreating others, at one point in time you will encounter mistreatment. If you have been blessing others, at one point you shall be blessed.

This is what Jesus was referring to when he said, "Give and it shall be given to you; good measure, pressed down, and shaken together, and running over shall men give into your bosom. For with the same measure that ye mete withal it shall be measured to you again" (Luke 6:38). Notice Jesus says you will not reap the same measure you sow, but it will be in multiplied form.

Jesus said while still talking about this law that you should do to others whatever you want to be done to you.

This is one of the reasons why I do my best to treat people well, because I don't want other people to mistreat me. If you don't want people to abuse you, don't go around abusing other people. If you don't want people to embarrass you, don't go around embarrassing other people. If you don't want people to humiliate you, don't go around humiliating other people, because the Bible says we shall reap whatsoever we are sowing.

The Bible says, "A man that hath friends must show himself friendly" (Proverbs 18:24). Some people wonder why they have no friends. You cannot have friends if you are not a friendly person. Whatever you sow, you will reap, but in multiplied form.

Look at the life of Mordecai in the book of Esther. One day while sitting at the gate, he overheard two men plotting to kill the king, and he went and warned him. He could have chosen to mind his own business and to keep quiet about the matter. Nothing was immediately done to repay him for this good deed by the king, but later when his life and that of the Jews hung in the balance, God caused the king to read the book of remembrance, and he was honored at this critical time. He was reaping what he had sown years earlier.

Look at Jonathan. He refused to join his father, King Saul, to mistreat David, even though it seemed the natural thing to do. Later, when Jonathan died, David treated his lame son Mephibosheth well. He brought him to the palace and fed him at his own table.

Look at Abigail—she refused to side with her husband, Nabal, in mistreating David, even though at that time David was a mere fugitive. When Nabal died unexpectedly, David took her in as his wife. She became the wife of a king. She became a queen because she planted good seeds. Watch whatever you are sowing in your words and actions.

The Bible mentions two types of sowing I would like us to look at. It says, "For he that soweth to his flesh, shall of the flesh reap corruption; but that he that soweth to the Spirit, shall of the Spirit reap life everlasting" (Galatians 6:8). Sowing to the flesh means following the evil desires of your flesh and sowing to the spirit means following the godly desires of your recreated spirit. These are very important areas of sowing with far reaching repercussions. As I said earlier we are sowing all the time many times unconsciously.

Another very important area of sowing is with our words. We need to realize that words are seeds that we reap from, as we saw earlier that we shall get whatever we are saying.

The reason why many people are not conscious about the operation of this law of sowing and reaping is because there is always a time span between when the seed is sown and when it's fully grown and ready for harvest.

Ecclesiastes says, "... because sentence against an evil work is not executed speedily therefore the heart of the sons of men is fully set in them to do evil" (Ecclesiastes 8:11). What this scripture is saying is that because people who do evil many times don't experience immediate punishment, many of them just continue doing this evil. Some of these people assume, falsely though, that God does not mind what they are doing. Pay day, however, is always guaranteed, unless there is total repentance and complete turning around.

The Bible says God:

> ... will render to everyman according to his deeds. To them who by patient continuance in well doing seek for glory and honor and immortality, eternal life; but unto them that are contentious and do not obey the truth but obey unrighteousness indignation and wrath. Tribulation and anguish upon every soul of man that doeth evil of the Jew first and also of the Gentiles. But glory, honor. and peace to everyman that worketh good, to the Jew first and also to the Gentile. For there is no respect of persons with God.
>
> Romans 2:6–11

Because God is not a respecter of persons, this spiritual law of sowing and reaping is applicable to everybody, and the harvest will always come at the appointed time.

We read in the book of Genesis, "... while the Earth remaineth, seed time and harvest and cold and heat and summer and winter and day and night shall not cease"

(Genesis 8:22). This law is going to always work as long as this earth remains.

The Bible, as I mentioned earlier, warns us not to deceive ourselves about the operation of this law. Many people, however, don't listen to this admonition and "deceive themselves." They keep sowing bad seeds and expect to reap a good harvest. They keep sowing strife and expect to reap a harvest of peace in their lives. People keep sowing evil and expect something good to come their way.

Some people don't sow at all and expect to harvest where they have not sown. This is mere self-deception. Learn to sow seeds on purpose that reflect the type of harvest you want to reap.

Others claim that this law works in other areas but does not work concerning money. This is far from the truth. Many of these people just do not have the faith to give or sow money. It takes faith to give money.

The Bible says in Hebrews, "By faith Abel offered unto God a more excellent sacrifice than Cain by which he obtained witness that he was righteous God testifying of his gifts: and by it he being dead yet speaketh" (Hebrews 11:4). Notice here that it took faith for Abel to make this offering. He knew that God was going to reward him for it. It was not simply a matter of giving to God; he was expecting something in return as the Word of God promises. So unlike his brother, he gave his best.

Some people even teach that it's selfish or greedy to give and expect God to give you back. That we should only give to meet needs of people and because of our love for Jesus Christ.

It's good to give because of the love of Christ and to help people with their needs, but giving with expectation shows that one has faith in God and his Word. It's actually God who promises to return our seeds sown in multiplied form, so he cannot be offended by one giving with the expectation of a return.

It's like saying God will be angry at a farmer who plants maize in a garden expecting to get a bigger harvest of maize. Actually, he challenges us to prove him in this area.

The Bible says that without faith we cannot please God—see Hebrews 11 verse 6. So it's not only about you getting money, but it's actually more about pleasing God by believing him. God is the one who gives us "power to get wealth." Certainly, he is the one who enriched Solomon who is said to have been the richest man in the world. Even Abraham's wealth came from God.

In 2 Corinthians, Paul says, "...he which soweth sparingly shall reap also sparingly; and he which soweth bountifully shall reap also bountifully" (2 Corinthians 9:6). Here Paul is talking about giving of material things, which includes money. God is also interested in our material prosperity.

God, in the Bible, has something to say about our finances and how we can multiply them. God more than anybody else, knows the importance of money to us in this world and has a lot to say about it in his Word.

Notice also here that the size of your harvest will depend on the measure to which you apply this law.

I believe that one of the reasons why there is a lot of lack and need of finances in the body of Christ is that we have been slack to apply this law. People have applied this law all right in the area of finances but in small measure. Some are even having difficulties in giving the tithe to the Lord. This law will, however, always work, whether we believe in it or not. "Whatsoever a man sows that shall he also reap."

The Bible exhorts us in the book of Galatians, " ... let us not be weary in well doing for in due season we shall reap if we faint not. As we have therefore opportunity let us do good unto all men especially unto them who are of the house hold of faith" (Galatians 6:9–10). Don't give up; pay day is coming.

What a tremendous law that we can take advantage of. Even though we were born in abject poverty, this law can help us attract money in our life. This is a sure way to overcome poverty in our life. We can change our destiny by using this law.

Law of Seed Faith

I would like to call the next law I am going to discuss in this book the law of seed faith. This law is similar to the law of sowing and reaping but somewhat different. This law says that you can use what you have to create what you don't have.

I sometimes refer to this law as the law of crisis because it's the law that can bail you out in a time of crisis. It's the law to use when you are stuck, when you have nowhere to turn. We saw in the last chapter the law of sowing and reaping. In this law of sowing and reaping our harvest is determined largely by God. We sow by faith according to his word and expect him to multiply and increase us in the best way he sees fit.

We most of the time receive a multiplied harvest, similar in kind to that which we have sown because the Bible says, "Let the earth bring forth grass, the herb yielding seed, and the fruit tree yielding fruit after his kind, whose seed is in itself, upon the earth: and it was so" (Genesis 1:11). Every seed reproduces a multiplied form of its kind. So when we sow money we get money back but in multiplied form. When we saw love we are loved back. When we sow help then some other person comes along and helps us, etc.

Sometimes God gives us a harvest in the area of our most pressing need. Also our harvest depends mostly on the measure that we mate because the Bible says that "for with the same measure that ye mate withal it shall be measured to you again" (Luke 6:38). What we get back is directly proportional to what we give. It may for example be out of the ordinary for someone to get one million us dollars for a seed of one thousand us dollars. On the contrary it may be quite normal, for a person who lets say, has sown six hundred thousand us dollars to receive back one million us dollars because this is a more proportionate measure. Of course, the measure also depends on the value one attaches to the seed sown.

The main difference between seed faith and the law of sowing and reaping is that in the law of sowing and reaping the harvest is largely determined by God according to his wisdom and judgment. With seed faith, however, one sows for a particular need. He sows with a specific harvest in mind. With seed faith the sower plays a significant part in determining the specific harvest he or she is to receive. When one sows seed faith, he or she needs to inform God what is being sown for.

It's like when we pray we have a certain specific answer to our prayer we are expecting. In this case we plant the seed of prayer and expect a specific harvest of answered prayer.

In seed faith also the harvest may be disproportionate or incomparable to the seed sown. For example you may sow a seed of finances but expect a harvest of protection or healing. You may sow a seed of finances and expect a harvest of salvation of a loved one. One brother sowed what he called a battle seed. He was in the midst of a battle or confrontation with some people when the Holy Spirit led him to sow a battle seed. When he obeyed and sowed this seed God immediately caused this war to cease.

Why does God heal someone after sowing a financial seed? The answer lies in faith. If he does this by faith, God will honor it as an act of faith and help the person sowing. In the Bible Jesus told people to do certain actions which my disquiet some people. God honored these instructions because they helped people to release their faith.

You see, money represents life in this world. We need it to buy food, pay for shelter, etc. It's not easy to give it away unless one has faith. Even conmen or people who don't understand the operation of this law can initiate miracles when they tell people to give in faith to God and expect a miracle. You see, God does not consider the action of the conman but the faith of the sower in performing such miracles. So both true financial deliverers and people just out to get money can unleash God's miracle working power if they can cause people to give in faith to God expecting a certain miracle. This does not mean, of course, that God approves what the conman is doing, but he will respect the law of seed faith when it's applied by the unsuspecting believer. It also means that no one can con you if you are giving to God, because he is the one to reward your faith.

For seed faith to work, one must sow or give what I would like to call a sacrificial seed. Not every seed will work as seed faith. A sacrificial seed is one that is sown out of need, not out of abundance. You must sow sacrificially for God to notice it as seed faith. The key to seed faith is to get the attention of God by your action.

One day, while seated at the treasury of the temple, Jesus saw people putting their offerings in the offering basket. He said the lady who put in two mites had given the most because she had given out of her want. Others had given out of their abundance see Mark 12:41–44. Hers was therefore a sacrificial seed although we cannot tell if it was seed faith.

King David refused to give to the Lord a sacrifice that did not cost him—see 1 Chronicles 21:24. He was being given by Ornan free sacrifices to offer. A sacrificial seed will cost you. This is the type of seed that will work as seed faith.

There is power in sacrificing to God. One day King Solomon sacrificed one thousand burnt offerings, and that night at Gibeon, God appeared to him and asked him to ask whatever he wanted—see 1 Kings 3:4–5. It was not a coincidence that God appeared to him the very night he offered this huge sacrifice. A lady in the Bible poured expensive perfume upon Jesus to prepare him for his burial, and Jesus said her fame would go throughout the earth. Some people present saw it as a waste but Jesus saw it as a sacrificial seed.

When Abraham was ready to sacrifice his son, Isaac, the Bible says that God swore upon himself an oath to confirm to Abraham the promises he had given him earlier—see Genesis 22:16–18. Of course, you must realize that God does not need to swear anything to anybody, because his word is good enough.

I will never forget it all the days of my life. One time several years ago, I boarded a British Airways plane to Los Angeles, California, where I was to attend a five-day Christian conference. At the end of the conference, I planned to spend two and a half more months in the USA preaching and believing God to raise funds for his work we are doing in Africa.

I paid for the conference expenses (that is the registration and hotel accommodations) while still in Uganda. After paying for the ticket (the money was borrowed), I only had one hundred US dollars left on me. I had no family and knew no one in California. I expected to live by faith while in the States. I only had that raw faith that David had when he confronted Goliath.

Just as we were about to board the connecting flight at London's Heathrow Airport, a security man with British Airways approached me and asked me some questions. On realizing that I had only one hundred dollars on me, and that I planned to spend three months in the USA, he asked me to follow him. In the meantime, the plane I was to take left for the States. He took me back to the immigration desk, where he complained that I was going to be deported at Los Angeles because I had very little money on me yet planned to spend a long time in the States.

British Immigration told him, however, that was none of their business. They told him that since my papers were in order they saw no reason why I should not proceed with my journey. This man apologized to me and put me on the next flight to Los Angeles, which was three hours later.

On arrival at Los Angeles, sure enough as this gentleman predicted, immigration at Los Angeles decided to deport me when they learned that I had only one hundred dollars and planned on spending three months in the USA. They informed me that in the USA, one hundred dollars would last me only one day.

They took me to a large room where I found many others waiting to be deported. From time to time security personnel would come to escort those whose plane was ready to go. After some time, a giant of a man entered the room. He seemed to walk aimlessly in the room until he spotted my documents (ticket, passport, and a book I had written called *Knowing the Secret of God's Power*) lying on the counter in the room. I saw him opening my book and start to read it. Then I saw his face smiling. He came to me and asked me whether I was the author of that book. He asked me a few other questions and told me to enter the U.S.A. I think he was the boss of the people who were deporting me, because they all seemed to respect him and the decision he had solely taken.

I entered the U.S.A., but still my financial situation had not changed. I used fourteen dollars to pay for a shuttle bus to Anaheim Convention Center where the conference was to take place and where I was booked to stay for the conference.

On one night during this conference, one preacher announced, just before he took the offering, that he believed that God was challenging us to sow sixty-five dollars in exchange for a financial miracle. I had not planned to give anything at this meeting since I had very little on me, but this preacher's bold declaration caught my attention because I clearly needed a financial a miracle.

Soon they started passing the offering plate. I had to decide quickly. I took God's offer. I reached in my pocket counted sixty-five dollars and folded it in my palms. I explained to God that I badly needed a breakthrough on this trip to the States and then dropped it on the offering plate. I felt like the widow of Zarephath giving her last plate of food.

At the end of the meeting an elderly lady, who was staying in an assisted living apartment and who had become our friend in the course of this meeting took me in and another pastor friend from Africa for a few days because she was not allowed to host guests, especially those of the opposite sex. The next Sunday she drove me to a big African-American church. My pastor friend knew a distant relative he went to be with.

We attended with her the service, and at the end she requested to see the pastor. She was referred to the assistant pastor to whom she explained my plight. The assistant pastor politely explained to her that they could not assist me because they did not know I was coming. He quoted the scripture that says that let everything be done decently and in order.

What happened next took me by surprise. The elderly sister who had brought me started shouting at the pastor asking, "What sort of church is this?" She told the pastor that if her, a white lady, could keep me in her assisted living apartment, how could such a big church, moreover of the same racial background as I was, say they could not help me?

The pastor, on realizing that this lady was causing a scene at the church (we were standing in the church lobby) and that believers coming out of the auditorium had started wondering what was going on, promised the lady that they were going to assist me. She then prayed for me a blessing and left. As soon as she left the pastor scribbled a few numbers of homeless shelters and asked me to call them and see if they could help and drove off.

I never bothered to call. I took my small bag, boarded a bus on the street outside the church not knowing where I was going, but surrounded by the peace of God that passes all understanding. At one point when the bus stopped I got off and started walking on the street. I saw another church and could hear people singing. They had begun their Sunday evening service. I entered that church that welcomed me and gave me food and a place to stay.

I met the pastor the next day on Monday. To my surprise he asked me to preach for him the next day Tuesday in the evening service. They took an offering for me of about five hundred dollars. Before I left the U.S.A. I was invited to preach again at that church.

Another pastor from another church had visited with them that Tuesday evening service, and he invited me to speak for him next Sunday. It went on and on. I got invitations to speak in over ten churches. I shipped back home a brand new PA system for our church in Uganda. I paid the ticket off and went back home loaded with blessings, all in the space of about two and half months, because I believed in my God, and I sowed a seed of faith in my time of crisis.

The Bible says, "Daniel was taken up out of the den, and no manner of hurt was found upon him, because he believed in his God" (Daniel 6:23). I know things would have turned out differently had I not planted that seed. Things would have turned out to be a lot harder than they were. Seed faith is not a myth. It's something that can bail you out in your time of crisis.

The Bible talks about several other people who sowed a seed of faith in their time of crisis, expecting God to bail them out. For example, there is Hannah, who promised to give God a son if only God would let her conceive this son—see 1 Samuel 1 verse 11. God accepted the terms.

The widow of Zarephath gave away her last plate of food expecting God to save her and her son from starvation, and she miraculously survived the terrible famine.

King David gave an offering on the threshing of Ornan and stopped the plague killing people in the land, and the list goes on.

When Jesus multiplied bread and fish to feed thousands of people, he asked his disciples to first find out what was available, which he used to perform this multiplication miracle. You can use what you have to get what you don't have. So if you are stuck in a crisis take an inventory of what you have. It can bail you out if you sow it in a faith.

Law of the Spirit of Life and the Law of Sin and Death

For the law of the Spirit of life in Christ Jesus hath made me free from the law of sin and death. For what the Law could not do in that it was weak through the flesh God sending his own Son in the likeness of sinful flesh, and for sin, condemned sin in the flesh; that the righteousness of the law might be fulfilled in us who walk not after the flesh but after the Spirit

For they that are after the flesh do mind the things of the flesh; but they that are after the Spirit the things of the Spirit. For to be carnally minded is death but to be spiritually minded is life and peace

Romans 8:2–6

In these verses of scripture, the Bible mentions two laws, namely the law of the spirit of life and the law of sin and death.

I would like to talk about these two laws in conjunction because the Bible does so.

The law of the spirit of life simply states that whenever you follow the leading of the Holy Spirit, you will flow in the life of God.

On the other hand, the law of sin and death says that whenever you follow your evil fleshly desires, you will be on the path that leads to death and destruction. So in these two laws we find life versus death.

In the beginning God warned the first man, Adam, together with his wife, Eve, not to eat of the tree of the knowledge of good and evil. He told them that they could eat of all other trees apart from this one. When they ate of this tree at the instigation of the devil, there was no immediate visible physical death. They of course immediately experienced a spiritual death, which separated them from God, but from a natural point of view, they seemed to be "alive and kicking." Sooner than later, however, they started together with their family members to conduct funeral ceremonies.

Sin will always result in death or in things we associate with death like pain, sickness, sorrow, and tears. It may be sweet or pleasurable for some time; the Bible talks about the "pleasures of sin for a season," but eventually it will turn bitter.

Conversely, following the Holy Spirit will always result in life and things we associate with life like joy, peace, success, blessings, etc.

The Bible teaches us that the real us, the inner man or our spirit being, is in a tug of war with the flesh. Both the Holy Spirit and the flesh want to lead us. The Holy Spirit leads us into life and the flesh into death. The choice is ours as to who we will let to lead us.

The Bible says, "... as many as a led by the Spirit of God they are the Sons of God" (Romans 8:14). It also says, "... to be carnally minded is death; but to be spiritually minded is life and peace" (Romans 8:6).

The one of the two we mind or think about will guide us to our destination. One leads us into *Zoe* or the God-kind of life and the other into death.

The Bible calls the Holy Spirit the Spirit of life. In the beginning he hovered upon the earth, and it was formless; when God spoke, the Holy Spirit started giving the earth the beautiful form it has today.

The book of Job says, "... the Spirit of God has made me and the breath of the Almighty hath given me life" (Job 33:40. The Holy Spirit will always lead you in paths of life and life more abundantly. He is the giver of life.

Conversely, the flesh will always lead you into death, loss, and failure. In the short run it may even appear as if you are gaining, but in the long run you will start noticing the failure.

The reason we have so many unhappy and frustrated Christians is that many in the body of Christ are not submitting to the leading of the Holy Spirit. Others have not learnt the art of being led by the Holy Spirit. We saw earlier, in the chapter talking about the law of recognition, how the Holy Spirit may lead us or speak to us.

We cannot attract those outside to join us if they see us leading unhappy, miserable lives. We are supposed to go through life, despite the challenges, with a song in our mouth and a spring in our walk.

Following the Holy Spirit in our daily walk will result in God infusing his energy and joy in us. Obeying the law of the spirit of life will help you lessen the pain and heartbreaks, which are in this fallen world and put a new song in your mouth.

You will start finding the Christian walk enjoyable instead of boring, and you will start sleeping like a baby, for God "gives his beloved sleep," the scripture says. Don't allow the devil to deceive you with his gifts. They may be sweet in the mouth but eventually will be more bitter than wormwood.

The Bible says in Proverbs, "There is a way that seems right unto a man; but the end thereof are the ways of death" (16:25).

Jesus in the book of Matthew chapter 7 verses 13–14 told us, "Enter ye in at the straight gate: for wide is the gate, and broad is the way, that leadeth to destruction, and many there be which go in thereat: Because strait is the gate, and narrow is the way which leadeth unto life, and few there be that find it" (Matthew 7:13–14).

There are clearly two ways that are available to man in this world. One is wide and broad and full of the fleshly pleasures of this world, and it's a one-way ticket to hell.

The other is small and narrow and full of godly sacrifices. This is the way to heaven and life. It's the way of the cross. It's the way the Holy Spirit (the spirit of life) is leading us.

The sad thing is that few people find this way. Unfortunately, most people are traveling the broad way of the flesh, which leads to destruction. Most people are carnally minded and are being led by their evil fleshly desires. They are the "living dead" as it were. They are operating under the law of sin and death instead of the law of the spirit of life.

The Bible says that Moses, when he grew up, refused to be called the son of pharaoh's daughter. It goes on to say that he refused to enjoy the "pleasures of sin for a season" but rather chose to suffer affliction with the people of God the Jews who were slaves at that time.

The Bible says that he esteemed "the reproach of Christ greater riches than the treasures in Egypt: for had respect unto the recompense of the reward" (Hebrews 11:26).

What a wise man, and what a wise choice! He saw through the lies of the devil. The reproach of Christ would eventually be more rewarding than all the riches of Egypt that the devil was offering him.

Sin and the flesh have no lasting reward. Their rewards are short lived and will sooner than later turn bitter. Things will start going sour, and you will live a life of regret.

The law of the spirit of life has made us free from the law of sin and death. You need not follow the bad law of sin and death. Many people are making the wrong choice of following this law. We see this all the time in nightclubs, on beaches, in pubs, etc., where people think they are having fun when actually they are destroying themselves.

Law of Multiplication

I would like to call the next law I want to discuss in this book the law of multiplication. This law says that in order for one to multiply and increase one has to first die one way or the other. This law is in many ways similar to the law of process we saw earlier but somewhat different.

Jesus, in the book of John, says, "…except a corn of wheat fall into the ground and die it abideth alone but if it die it bringeth forth much fruit" (12:24).

According to this scripture, for a corn of wheat to multiply it has first to die. If you are to increase, you have to die one way or the other. The death process is painful but eventually brings about increase.

We read in the book of Exodus:

> Now there arose up a new King over Egypt, which knew not Joseph. And he said unto his people, behold the people of the children of Israel are more and mightier than we. Come on let us deal wisely with them; lest they multiply and it come to pass that when there falleth out any war, they join also unto our enemies, and fight against us, and so

get them out of the land. Therefore they did set over them task masters to afflict them with their burdens. And they built for Pharaoh treasure cities Pithom and Raamses. But the more they afflicted them the more they multiplied and grew. And they were grieved because of the children of Israel.

Exodus 1:6–12

In these verses of scripture we read that the new pharaoh, who ascended the throne in Egypt and who did not know Joseph, wanted to cut Israel short by persecuting them. The Bible says, however, that the more he did this, the more the children of Israel multiplied. Clearly this Pharaoh did not know this law of multiplication; otherwise he would have not persecuted Israel in the first place because this had an opposite effect to what he hoped to happen. It boomeranged on him.

In the book of Deuteronomy chapter 8, God says that he led the children of Israel purposely in the wilderness in order to give them a great end. Moses in the book of Deuteronomy, told the children of Israel not to forget God who:

…led thee through that great and terrible wilderness wherein were fiery serpents and scorpions and drought where there was no water, who brought thee forth water out of the rock of flint. Who fed thee in the wilderness with manna which thy fathers knew not, that he might humble thee and that he might prove thee to do thee good at thy latter end.

Deuteronomy 8:15–16

In these scripture verses, the Bible says that God led the children of Israel through the terrible wilderness, in order to do them good at the end.

In the book of Deuteronomy Moses also tells the children of Israel to:

> ... remember all the way which the Lord thy God led thee these forty years in the wilderness to humble thee and to prove thee to know what was in thine heart whether though wouldest keep his commandments or no." And he humbled thee and suffered thee to hunger, and fed thee with manna, which thou knewest, not neither did thy fathers know; that he might make thee know that man doth not live by bread only, but by every word that proceedeth out of the mouth of the Lord does man live."
>
> Deuteronomy 8:2–3

In these scriptures, God, through Moses, explains to the children of Israel why he purposely led them through the wilderness. God first led them through the wilderness to enable them to bear the "fruit of the Holy Spirit."

The Bible says that he wanted to teach them humility. This would result in them getting more grace. The scriptures say that God gives more grace. The scriptures also say that God resists the proud but gives more grace to the humble. Humility attracts more of the grace of God in our lives. Remember: it's the grace of God that increases us in every way.

In the book of James, we are told to "count it all joy when you fall in divers temptations. Knowing this that the trying of your faith worketh patience. But let patience have her perfect work that you may be perfect and entire wanting nothing" (1:2–4).

According to this text of scriptures, suffering and the trials of life help us to bear the fruit of the Holy Spirit. This results in God adding other things to us, because the Bible tells us to "seek ye first the Kingdom of God and his righteousness, and all these things shall be added unto you" (Matthew 6:33).

When you find the kingdom of God and his righteousness, certain things will be added unto you. So suffering directly or indirectly brings about increase in our fruits of righteousness and inevitably also our material things.

Another thing Moses says that God was teaching the children of Israel in the wilderness was that man shall not live by bread alone but by every " ... word that proceedeth out of the mouth of the Lord" (Deuteronomy 8:3).

God was actually teaching them how to live by faith. When you learn to live your life according to the Word of God then you have learned to leave by faith.

The Bible says that the just shall live by faith. We are not only saved by faith, but we have to live by faith in our daily walk.

The reason why many believers are failing to overcome the world is that they have not mastered this all-important lesson of living by faith. Many believers only know how to live by sight in their daily walk.

Many believers feel as if it's the end of the world when their balance in the bank is at zero or when all of a sudden they become jobless. It's a good thing to have a well paying job and to have a good amount of money in the bank, but even without these things, God is able to take care of you comfortably if you learn to live by faith. God's provisions are not limited to our jobs and bank accounts. Mordecai told Esther that if she refused to help them, the help of God was going to come from another source. So if you are living by faith in God, you don't have only one source of help.

Jesus told us that in the world we shall confront problems but to be of good cheer because he had overcome the world. In the world, they are problems, but if we are living by faith, we can walk in the victory of Jesus.

We are also told in the book of 1 John, "… whatsoever is born of God overcometh the world…" (5:4)

The Bible goes on to say in the next verse, "… this is the victory which overcometh the world even our faith" (1 John 5:5). When the Bible here talks about the world they are talking about life's problems.

Many believers are falling flat on their faces in the face of life's problems because they don't know how to live by faith. It's our faith in God that can overcome the problems in this world. Many have been overcome by life's problems, and some have even died prematurely because they don't know how to apply their faith.

You can best learn how to live by faith by going through the wilderness or by going through life's challenges. We need to be taught faith in the church; but as we confront these challenges and apply the things we have learned, that's when we can really develop our faith until we get faith to move mountains. As we start living by faith or by the Word of God we start experiencing increase in every way. That's why this spiritual law says that you increase by dying.

There is another side to suffering. It can bring about increase in our life if we go through it without murmuring or complaining but put our trust in God. That's why the Apostle Paul says he reached a point where he "gloried in tribulation"—see Romans 5 verse 3. He goes on to say, " ... tribulation worketh patience and patience experience; and experience hope" (Romans 5:3–4).

In 2 Corinthians he says, " ... therefore I take pleasure in infirmities, in reproaches in necessities, in persecutions in distresses for Christ sake: for when I am weak then am I strong" (12:10). When we are weak, then we are strong or more anointed and we can do more for the Lord.

I must confess, I don't know of many Christians who delight in suffering like the Apostle Paul is saying in these scriptures. This is because many have probably not discovered the other side of suffering, which is the side that brings about increase in our life.

Many of us are always just griping and complaining when going through the problems in life. However, because God wants to do us good at the end, he allows us to go through this path of suffering.

In Psalm 66, the Bible says, "For thou O God hast proved us: thou hast tried us as silver is tried. Thou broughtest us into the net; thou laidst affliction upon our loins. Thou hast caused men to ride over our heads; we went through fire and through water; but thou broughtest us out into a wealthy place" (66:10–12).

The way to the wealthy place is via the trials of life, thus the law that multiplication comes about by dying. The people in the above scriptures went through a lot of reproach and problems, but they ended up in a wealthy place.

Law of Vision

I would like to call the next law I want to discuss in this book the law of vision. This law says that you will only be able to attain that which you see with your eyes of faith. You will only get that for which you have vision. If you can see it, you can get it. If you get a continual visual, then you know it will materialize sooner or later.

God told Abraham in Genesis, " ... all the land which thou seest, to thee will I give it, and to thy seed forever" (13:15).

In Genesis the Bible says that God brought Abraham "forth abroad and said look now toward Heaven, and tell the stars, if thou be able to number them: and he said unto him, so shall thy seed be" (15:5).

In both of these incidents God was trying to inspire Abraham's vision and thereby his faith, because you can only get that which you can see according to this law.

You will only become like what you see yourself to be or like your self-image. When you really believe in something, it starts forming mental images in your mind and also in your spirit. Real faith starts producing visions. You will only attain the level you see yourself attaining, and you will only receive those things you see yourself receiving. You will only go as far as your vision.

God is limitless. God is able to do anything, but he can only do for you what you see him doing. It's only your vision that can limit him. Vision is very important because it sets parameters of what God can do for you.

One of the saddest statements is found in Psalm 78 verse 41, and it says that the children of Israel "limited the Holy One of Israel." They saw a smaller picture of what God could actually do for them.

The Bible says in the Psalms, "...they spake against God; they said, can God furnish a table in the wilderness? Behold he smote the rock that the waters gushed out, and the streams overflowed; can he give bread also? Can he provide flesh for his people?" (Psalm 78:19–20). These people put a limit on what God could do for them. You can limit God by your vision.

Your vision is what you see yourself doing and becoming. You need to enlarge your vision if you want God to do for you mighty things. Our vision is shaped by God's Word to us and also by what we have seen God do in the lives of others.

God, in the book of Numbers, told Moses to pick twelve people to go and spy out the Promised Land. He wanted them to see the flow of milk and honey that was in this land.

Unfortunately, however, ten of the twelve spies focused on the giants instead. They saw the picture from the wrong angle, as it were. They were inevitably defeated.

These people saw themselves as grasshoppers instead of giant killers. These people, the Bible says, brought an evil report to the congregation and infected them with this report.

Two of the twelve, Joshua and Caleb, saw things from God's point of view and were able to possess the land flowing with milk and honey.

If you are to succeed in life you need to have the right vision of yourself. You need to see yourself as God sees you. God's vision of you is found in his word. Many times in the Bible people saw themselves differently from the way God was seeing them. God had to help correct their vision before he could use them.

Jeremiah saw himself only but a child in Jeremiah chapter 1 verse 6, but God saw him as a prophet to the nations—see verse 5.

Gideon saw himself as a vulnerable, impoverished, good for nothing captive, but God saw him as a "mighty man of valor"—see Judges chapter 6 verses 12–15.

Peter saw himself as a worthless sinner and told Jesus to depart from him, but Jesus saw him as a "fisher of men." Paul saw himself as chief among the sinners and the least of all the apostles, but God saw him as a mighty apostle to the Gentiles.

At one time Moses saw himself as a helpless fugitive looking after his father-in-law's sheep on the backside of the desert. It took God quite some effort to convince him to go and deliver the children of Israel from Egypt. God had to go out of his way to convince Moses that with him he was a mighty deliverer.

What you see will determine whether you will get the victory or be defeated in your battles.

The Bible says, concerning Moses in the book of Hebrews, "By faith he forsook Egypt not fearing the wrath of the King for he endured as seeing him who is invisible" (11:27). Moses by faith defied the pharaoh of Egypt, the most powerful ruler at the time, because he saw God the "Invisible One" with him, in this conflict. This vision of God, gave him courage in this severe conflict, and he had the confidence that God was going to see him through. Notice here that this vision of Moses drove out his fears. Vision is a fear killer.

Even Jesus saw the "Invisible One" in his greatest trial when he went to hell on our behalf to overcome the powers of darkness. Jesus says in the book of Acts:

> I foresaw the Lord always before my face. For he is on my right hand, that I should not be moved: Therefore did my heart rejoice and my heart was glad, moreover also my flesh shall rest in hope: Because thou will not leave my soul in hell, neither wilt thou suffer thine Holy One to see corruption.
> Acts 2:25–27

This was the confession of Jesus when he went to hell for you and me. He says that because he continuously saw the Lord before his face, even while in hell, he rejoiced in his heart, and his tongue was glad. He was actually praising the Lord right in the middle of hell.

He refused to be moved by hell and its terrors, because the Lord he was seeing was going to help him. God was not going to leave his soul in hell and was not going to allow him to see corruption. The vision of God he was seeing while in hell encouraged him and saw him through this trial.

Paul saw a vision of an angel of the "Invisible One" in the midst of a terrible storm, when he was being taken as a prisoner to Rome. The Bible says in the book of Acts:

> ...after a long abstinence Paul stood forth in the midst of them, and said, Sirs you should have hearkened unto me and not have loosed from Crete and to have gained this harm and loss. And now I exhort you to be of good cheer: for there shall be no loss of any man's life among you, but of the ship. For there stood by me this night the Angel of the Lord whose I am and whom I serve. Saying fear not Paul; thou must be brought before Caesar: and, lo, God has given thee all them that sail with thee.
>
> Acts 27:21–24

As a result of this vision he got the courage to break bread and eat and also encouraged the other fellow passengers to do the same—see verses 33–36.

I remember many years ago as a young pastor, demons attacked me and "whipped" me very badly. The devil took advantage of the fact that I was still a baby Christian and attacked me mercilessly. In the midst of this severe trial, I was asking the Lord to take me home to heaven all the time. One day after the evening service in the church where I had gone to take refuge, I prayed desperately a short prayer from Psalm 103 asking the Lord to pity me as a father pities his child. When I got off my knees I heard this voice speak to me audibly (at least it sounded to me) in my local language that I was going to see God that day. At the time I did not understand what this voice was talking about because my prayer was not to see a vision of God but to have him deliver me from this affliction.

When I left the altar where I had been praying and stepped on the floor of the church, the power of God hit me through my feet, and in seconds surged through my entire body. As it passed through my body, I involuntarily raised my hands and head toward heaven. I then saw the heavens open, and two words rushing to me like a mighty river. They were in English. The one in the lead was *Father* and the one following at the rear was *Jesus*.

I believe that God showed me this vision to encourage and sustain me until I received my total deliverance, which came sometime later.

Many people are defeated in their battles because they don't see the invisible one in the midst of their trails. They instead see the devil and how large their problems are.

Whatever you are going through, if you want to "crossover" to the other side, you need to keep on seeing the invisible one.

This is why Elisha the prophet prayed for his servant, in the book of 2 Kings, that God may open his eyes and enable him to see the reality of the situation. They had been besieged by the army of Syria.

The Bible says that God answered the prayer of Elisha and "opened the eyes of the young man; and he saw: and behold, the mountain was full of horses and chariots of fire round about Elisha" (2 Kings 6:17). They were more on their side than the side of the Syrians. This greatly encouraged this servant of Elisha. All the fear was expelled, and confidence set in because of this vision. Many times we are afraid unnecessarily because we can't see what's really going on in the spiritual realm.

God paints or forms these visions in our spirits and minds, as pictures of our future, to enable us grasp it with our faith and bring it into reality. Sometimes we paint these pictures ourselves and then grasp them with our faith so we can bring them into reality. Either way if we get to see it on a continuous basis we have a wonderful opportunity of getting it.

Our vision matters because it determines the height to which we can reach. Many people are living far below their potential because, not only are they carrying small visions, but wrong visions all together. We need to be pregnant with visions of God.

The devil is also good at giving people his own version of visions. He always wants you to see yourself dying or very poor or as a failure. Unfortunately, many people are hanging on these demonic visions some even mistaking them to be heavenly visions. You need to fight and get rid of these visions because if you hang on them, they will destroy you. Hang on to the heavenly visions. Paul told king Agrippa that he was not disobedient to the "heavenly vision."

The Bible says, "... where there is no vision the people perish ..." (Proverbs 29:18). Unless we get a vision of helping lost humanity, people will continue perishing every day. God has over the years been giving people visions to help them create a better future for themselves so he could use them to help others.

Joseph saw himself as a very important person long before he became a prime minister.

Paul the apostle started seeing himself as an apostle to the Jews, Gentiles, and kings on the very day of his conversion.

The prophetic word, if you can receive it is intended to give you a vision for the future. As you continue to play this vision in your mind and spirit you are bringing it closer to reality.

Law of Faith

I would like to call the next law I want to discuss in this book the law of faith. This law says that you will only believe in what you have heard. It's impossible to believe beyond what you have heard.

The Bible says in the book of Romans, "...faith cometh by hearing and hearing by the word of God" (Romans 10:17). So faith comes through the function of hearing. And it's our faith that causes us to receive from God.

In verse 14 the Bible asks, "How then shall they call on him whom they have not believed? And how shall they believe in him of whom they have not heard? And how shall they hear without a preacher?" (Romans 10:14).

Simply put you cannot believe in someone or something you have never heard about. You cannot believe in Jesus unless somebody has told you about him.

Hearing is a must for one to believe. Sight can enhance faith, but sight alone cannot create faith because what you are seeing has to be qualified or defined.

Jesus says in the book of Mark, "...if any man have ears to hear, let him hear" (Mark 4:23).

He goes on to say in verses 24–5, "...take heed what ye hear: with what measure ye mate it shall be measured to you: and unto you that hear shall more be given. For he that hath to him shall be given and he that hath not from him shall be taken even that which he hath" (Mark 4:24–25).

These scriptures are very revealing about the importance of hearing. The Bible here is not necessarily referring to your natural hearing function. It's mainly talking about your spiritual ears. Of course we know that many times your spiritual ears pick the signals or the words from your physical ears, so they are also important.

These scriptures first of all reveal that we receive from God through the hearing function. The Bible says here that more shall be given to the person who is hearing. God gives us whatever we need through what we are able to hear and believe in his Word because faith comes by hearing and hearing by the Word of God.

It's very important for us to hear the Word of God and to hear it correctly because it's the avenue God uses to bless us, heal us, and to give us whatever we need.

The Bible goes on to say that for those who are not hearing the word of God, that even that little they have received, from the little they have heard, will be taken away and given to those who are hearing. We should be careful what we are hearing because this will determine if we are to receive anything from God.

Secondly the above mentioned scriptures reveal to us that the amounts or quantities we receive from God are determined by the degree to which we are hearing. The Bible says that with the measure we mate out, the same measure will be used to mate out to us. Remember here the Bible is talking about hearing.

The more we attend to God's Word, the more we shall be able to receive from him. We need to give the word of God our attention, if we are to have our needs met. In the parable of the Sower, the fertile soils, that is those that were bearing fruit, bore this fruit in different proportions, that is "some thirty-fold, some sixty, and some a hundred" (Mark 4:20). This is because the degree to which we hear determines the degree to which we receive.

In the book of Galatians, the Apostle Paul asks the Galatians the method they applied to get their miracles. He asks them, "…he therefore that ministereth to you the Spirit and worketh miracles among you doeth he it by the works of the law or by the hearing of faith?" (Galatians 3:5).

He asks them because apparently they were backsliding from grace and faith and going back to getting righteousness through keeping the Law of Moses, a method that had refused to work in the first place.

The scriptures here reveal that God did miracles for the Galatians through the "hearing of faith." They were able to get these miracles because they heard and believed the word preached to them. This is the way God did miracles for the Galatians, and it's the way he will do them for you, that is through the hearing of faith.

When Philip went to preach the gospel in Samaria in the book of Acts. the Bible says, "the people with one accord gave heed unto those things which Philip spake hearing and seeing the miracles which he did" (Acts 8:6).

These people heard and saw the miracles. They heard the word talking about God's miracle working power, that's how they were able to see the miracles.

The Bible in the book of Acts says that while Paul was preaching, "... there sat a certain man at Lystra impotent in his feet, being a cripple from his mother's womb who never had walked" (Acts 14:8).

The Bible goes to say, "... the same heard Paul speak: who steadfastly beholding him and perceiving that he had faith to be healed, said with a loud voice, stand upright on thy feet. And he leaped and walked" (Acts 14:9–10). What made this man to walk, was his faith he got by hearing Paul preach.

After he got this faith it was written all over his face, so Paul did not wait for the time of the altar call. Right in the middle of the sermon he told him to stand up and walk. The reason why this man was able to walk is because he was attentive to what Paul was preaching, and this created faith in his heart which activated the miracle.

In the book of 2 Chronicles, the Queen of Sheba traveled a long journey to visit with King Solomon. She told King Solomon after her arrival, "... it was a true report which I heard in my own land, of thine acts and of thy wisdom" (9:50).

What she saw when she arrived at Solomon's court perfected her faith, but what she heard in her own land initiated this faith. It set her off on this journey. The Bible says that she went back with answers to all her difficult questions and that King Solomon gave her "all her desires."

Many people don't know how to receive miracles from God. It must be through the "hearing of faith." If you are to get something from God the first step is to hear and believe his word. What you hear determines what you are able to believe.

The reason why many people are not getting God's miracles is because they are trying to receive them without hearing his word first of all. Many are trying to believe God without believing in his Word, that's why they are falling flat on their faces. God and his Word are one, and God moves according to his Word. You cannot receive miracles independent of God's Word. You have to hear his Word prior to receiving your miracle, because this law says you can only believe that which you have heard.

Proverbs chapter 4 verse 20 tells us to attend to God's words and to incline our ears to his sayings. When we do this, the Bible says in verse 22, that these words will be life unto us and health to our flesh. For the Word of God to become life and health to us we have to be attentive to what it's saying.

The Bible says in John chapter 1 verse 14 that the Word of God became flesh. The Word of God in John chapter 2, at the wedding at Cana of Galilee, turned into wine when they had run out of drinks. For this to have happened, the servants had to first of all hear this word and to believe it. They had to obey the instructions of filling the water pots with water. For the Word of God to turn into whatever you need it to turn into, you must first hear it and then apply it; that's when a metamorphosis will occur.

First Corinthians chapter 14 verse 10 says that there are, it may be, so many kinds of voices in the world and none of them is without signification. They are many voices that want you to lend them your ears and to give them your time. What voice are you listening to?

Even the devil has a voice. Doubt too has a voice. What you hear and the way you hear it will determine what you believe, but also what you believe will be determined by what you have heard, because you can only believe that which you have heard. What we are hearing is very important. It can get us a miracle or it can curse us.

In the book of Numbers many of the children of Israel became destined to perish, because they chose to hear and believe the evil report of the ten spies.

If you are to avoid defeat you have to refuse to hear some voices that sometimes will be screaming at you.

The Bible says in Romans chapter 4 that by faith Abraham refused to consider his body, which was dead, and the deadness of Sarah womb. I am sure the devil tried to talk to him about this, but he turned him off. He refused to listen to this voice that wanted to talk to him about the state of his body and that of Sarah his wife. Had he hearkened to this voice of doubt, it would have defeated his faith.

You need to turn off your hearing when the devil is trying to use some people to plant doubt in your heart. This is why Jesus told Peter to "get behind me, Satan." The devil was trying to use him to plant doubt and fear in the life of Jesus. The reason why Eve was defeated in the garden of Eden is because she chose to listen to the devil.

You don't have to listen to everybody because sometimes it's not worth it. Sometime it will cost you to listen to some people. If it does not change your course of action, it may rob you of your peace of mind.

Some years ago in my country many believers were zealous to win the Muslims to Jesus, and one of the prominent preachers then said that he had received a vision in which the Lord had told him to study the Koran and to use it to win these Muslims to Jesus. Many other believers followed suit. They were walking around with a copy of the Koran in one hand and that of the Bible in another.

The Lord, however, advised me to stay away from this movement, which was very popular at that time. The reason he gave me was that faith comes by hearing and hearing by the Word. Faith in God comes by hearing the Word of God, and faith in the devil comes by hearing the word of the devil. The principle is the same because this is a spiritual law.

The believers who were studying the Koran, to supposedly win the Muslims, were unconsciously corrupting their faith by planting seeds of doubt in it because faith comes by hearing and hearing by the Word.

They were also other problems with this method. If you use the Koran to defend parts of the faith you are admitting the authenticity of this book. Also this type of gospel gendered a lot of strife because the Muslims felt that the preachers were desecrating their holy book.

Whereas these preachers were doing this in good faith and to glorify the name of Jesus, this method was clearly wrong. It far exceeded what Paul was talking about when he said to win the Jews he became like the Jews. To win people we can outwardly make attempts to identify with them but certainly not to adapt their theology.

The Lord revealed to me that there was enough power in the word of God to "win" anybody, Muslim or not, to Jesus Christ. God does not need to enlist the help of the Koran or any other religious book to win people to the Lord. His word is sufficient for the task.

We must, therefore, be careful about what we are hearing. If it's not profitable, we need to plug cotton wool in our ears. If it's profitable, we need to listen attentively to what is being said because this law says that we shall only be able to believe that we hear. What you keep on hearing will after sometime start registering with you.

Law of Possession

I would like to call the next law I want to discuss the law of possession. This law says that you will only possess that which you step into. God may want you to possess something, but you have to step into it in order to possess it.

You cannot possess something as a passive bystander or spectator. You have to be actively involved in order to possess what God will have you possess.

In the book of Joshua, the Bible says:

> Now after the death of Moses the servant of the Lord it came to pass that the Lord spake unto Joshua the son of Nun Moses' minister saying,
>
> Moses my servant is dead; now therefore arise, go over this Jordan, thou and all this people, unto the land which I do give to them, even to the children of Israel.
>
> Every place that the sole of your foot shall tread upon that have I given unto you, as I said unto Moses.
>
> Joshua 1:1–3

Notice in these verses of scripture that even though the Lord had given the children of Israel a certain amount of land, they had to tread in it in order for them to possess it. Even though God had potentially given it to them, they had to go for it in order for them to receive it.

In the book of Joshua the Bible says, "Now Joshua was old and stricken in years; and the Lord said unto him, thou art old and stricken in years and there remaineth yet much land to be possessed" (Joshua 13:1).

What God was telling Joshua was that he was running out of time. God had given him a lot of land to possess, but he had managed to possess only a part of that land and he had become very old and was about to die. God was encouraging him to go for more of this land so that he would not die a failure.

One can be said to die a failure if he or she dies without achieving what God wanted them to achieve.

The reason Joshua had not been able to possess this land was that it was not actually vacant when God gave it to him. This land had nations occupying it, which Joshua had to dislodge before he could take possession of it.

The Hittites, the Girgashites, the Amorites, the Canaanites, the Perizzites, the Hivites, and the Jebusites (the seven nations that occupied this land that were greater and mightier than Israel—see Deuteronomy Chapter 7 verse 1) were unwilling to give it up to the children of Israel without putting up a fight.

Joshua and the children of Israel had fought several battles to take the land they had managed to possess and had most probably gotten tired of fighting. They no longer had the will to fight. They were suffering from battle fatigue. For lack of will to fight, they became content with the status quo.

Many times we, like the children of Israel, are unwilling to fight for things God has given us that the devil is holding onto. We sometimes don't want to get involved because this can be inconvenient and costly. Getting involved may be humiliating and time consuming. We may be misunderstood by people and sometimes we may even lose our friends. We may be launching out in what appears to be a risky, uncertain, and foolhardy venture.

Unless we get involved, however, we cannot take hold of our possession or our inheritance because this law says that we can only possess those things we step into or get involved with.

We must be willing to put up a fight and dislodge the demons that are occupying our inheritance. We must get actively involved and take back what belongs to us, which the devil has stolen since the days of Adam. We will only be able to possess that land that we step into. God has given us these exceedingly great and precious promises, but we will only receive what we go for. The devil will also try to hinder us from receiving them.

In the book of Numbers, "…the Lord spake unto Moses saying vex the Midianites and smite them for they vex you with their wiles wherewith they have beguiled you in the matter of Peor, and in the matter of Cozbi, the daughter of a Prince of Midian, their sister, which was slain in the day of the plague for Peor's sake" (25:16–18).

In this chapter, the children of Israel were under attack by the devil. He was using the daughters of Moab to lead the children of Israel astray. The Bible says in Numbers, "And Israel abode in Shittim, and the people begun to commit whoredom with the daughters of Moab. And they called the people unto the sacrifice of their gods; and the people did eat and bowed down to their gods" (Numbers 25:1–3).

Because of this trespass, we are told that twenty-four thousand people of the children of Israel died from a plague inflicted upon them by the Lord as punishment (see verse 9).

The devil was trying to cut the children of Israel short by using the Midianites to tempt them to sin against the Lord. They were seducing them into sexual sin and involving them in the worship of Baal-Peor, a pagan god, which was idolatry. The Lord advised them to fight back and to vex the Midianites. You are not supposed to sit idly by and let the devil plunder you. You are supposed to do something about the devil.

We are told in 1 Peter to resist the devil "steadfastly in the faith" (5:9). We are also told in the book of James chapter 4 verse 7 to resist the devil, and he will flee from us if we do so. Notice in these verses of scripture it's you who is supposed to resist the devil using the authority God has given you, not God to do it for you.

It's up to us to get involved and cast the devil and his cohorts out using the weapons of our warfare. The Bible tells us:

> Finally, my brethren be strong in the Lord and the power of his might. Put on the whole armor of God that you may be able to stand against the wiles of the Devil. For we wrestle not against flesh and blood but against principalities, against powers against the rulers of the darkness of this world, against spiritual wickedness in high places. Wherefore take unto you the whole armor of God that ye may be able to withstand in the evil day and having done all to stand.
>
> Ephesians 6:10–13

The Bible then goes on to give us a list of this armor. We are told in verse 14, "... stand therefore having your loins girt about with truth" (Ephesians 6:14). Some versions of the Bible tell us here to put on the belt of truth. Why do we need to put on the belt of truth when dealing with the devil? This is because he is a liar and the father of lies. Conversely we are told in Hebrews chapter 6 verse 18 that it's impossible for God to tell a lie.

The Bible says that from the beginning the devil refused to abide in the truth, and the Bible goes on to say that there is no truth in him—see John 8 verse 44. This means that whenever the devil speaks out, all or most of what his saying are lies. A habitual liar, he tries to overcome you with these lies. So you must be equipped with the truth of God's word to counter the lies of the devil.

The Bible says that the law came by Moses, but grace and truth came by Jesus Christ—see John chapter 1 verse 17. Jesus says in the Bible that he is the way, the truth, and the life. So if you want to know the truth about God and his kingdom then you have to listen to Jesus. Conversely, if you want to be deceived about God and his kingdom then you listen to the devil.

The devil is deceiving people with all sorts of lies. He has told the atheists that there is no God out there but only empty space. Then he has told the religious people that there is God all right but that you can approach him any way you wish not necessarily the biblical way.

He can sometimes even be more subtle in his deceptions by using scriptures to deceive people, but in a distorted way. This was what he was trying to do when he told Jesus to jump from the highest pinnacle of the temple because it is "written He shall give his angels charge over thee to keep thee and in their hands they shall bear thee up lest at any time thou dash thy foot against a stone" (Luke 4:10–11).

Even though this scripture that the Devil quoted is there in the Bible, he was deliberately misinterpreting it to put Jesus in harm's way. Jesus saw through his lies and told him it's written you shall not tempt the Lord your God.

Even though God had promised angelic deliverance, he did not do so to those who endangered their lives on purpose, to prove a point to the devil. The devil wanted Jesus to break his legs by misrepresenting scriptures. So you must not only know the truth of God's Word, you must rightly divide this truth in order to counter the lies of the devil; otherwise you are no match against him.

We are also told in Ephesians chapter 6 verse 14 to put on the breastplate of righteousness.

This can have a double meaning. First of all, it's encouraging us to live right or to have a clean life. In the book of Ephesians we are told, "Be ye angry and sin not; let not the sun go down upon your wrath. Neither give place to the devil" (4:26–27). Not living correctly gives the devil a place in your life. When you continue unabated on the path of sin, you open a door for the devil in your life and remember he comes not but to steal, kill, and destroy.

Secondly, it means that you must recognize the gift of righteousness you are adorned with because you belong to Jesus. The Bible calls the devil the accuser of the brethren who is accusing them before our God day and night.

The devil loves to keep you under condemnation and guilt all the time because this can steal your peace and disorganize your life. This can also hinder your prayer life and also your fellowship with the heavenly father.

The devil wants to use it to make you afraid of the presence of God because he eventually wants to separate you with the heavenly Father. The reason why Adam and Eve were hiding after eating the forbidden fruit is that they were now afraid of the presence of a Holy God. That's what sin always does. It makes you uncomfortable in God's presence, and the devil knows this and tries to exploit it whenever he gets a chance to do so.

Understanding the gift of righteousness and salvation by grace not by works will keep your relationship with God going despite any weaknesses you may still be experiencing.

I must, however, be quick to add that this should not be a license to sin and that we should work on our weaknesses whatever they may be. The Bible tells us to "work out your salvation with fear and trembling" (Philippians 2:12). Even though God does not want us to sin he has provided for us forgiveness and an advocate Jesus to help us continue our relationship with him.

The other piece of armor we need to put on is to let our feet be "shod with the preparation of the gospel of peace" (Ephesians 6:15). The gospel brings about peace by driving away the demons which rob people of Gods peace.

The Bible calls the gospel the power of God that saves people. It's also the power of God that drives away demons from people lives. Whenever you preach the gospel you take the battle into the devil's backyard as it were. You shift from a defensive to an offensive position. As you preach the gospel, the devil leaves your backyard to defend his. So the first person to be delivered as the gospel is preached is the preacher.

The preacher is the first person to partake of God's peace. So if you are tormented by demons, just start sharing the good news of the gospel with your neighbors and friends and you will experience your own deliverance.

We are also told to adorn the shield of faith with which to quench the fiery darts of the devil. The devil cannot overrun a person who is standing in faith. In order for him to do, he has to first move that person out of the position of faith.

The fiery arrows they are talking about here are those of fear, worry, doubt, anger, etc., which are always the side effects of unbelief. The person who is standing in faith is always in a position of rest because the Bible says that those who believe have entered their rest. The place of rest is one where the peace of God is guarding your heart and mind in Christ Jesus. It's a place where you are unmovable and unshaken by whatever is going on. It's the best place to be in the midst of life's problem. It's a place where you can sleep in the midst of a storm like Jesus did.

The psalmist says, "God is our refuge and strength a very present help in trouble. Therefore we will not fear though the earth be removed, and the mountains be carried into the midst of the sea. Though the waters thereof roar and be troubled though the mountains shake with the swelling thereof. Selah" (Psalm 46:1). For someone not to fear in a catastrophe of such a magnitude is a clear testimony that they are standing in faith.

The devil really has no new tactics. He uses the same old tactics over and over again. He is trying to strike terror in your heart and make you anxious. He knows that an anxious person is not in faith and capable of doing anything.

The Bible also tells us in Ephesians chapter 6 to put on the helmet of salvation. In 1 Thessalonians chapter 5 verse 8 we are told the helmet represents the hope of salvation.

We of course were saved when we believed on the Lord Jesus, but in a sense our salvation will be consummated when the Lord returns and puts all his enemies under his feet. The Bible says the last enemy he will overcome is death. This will then put a complete end to the works of the devil.

The Bible tells us that the devil will first be chained and thrown into the bottomless pit for a thousand years see Revelation chapter 20. Then later after these years he will be judged and thrown in the lake of fire, which will be his eternal abode. In the book of Romans chapter 16 verse 20 we read that the God of peace shall bruise Satan under your feet shortly talking of the total annihilation of the devil in the lake of fire.

We must not lose sight of this salvation by putting on the Helmet of salvation. We must remember that one day all demonic oppression will come to an end.

Then also the Bible tells us to wield the sword of the Spirit, which is the Word of God. This is talking about the spoken Word of God or the Word of God on our lips or in our mouth.

The spoken word is a very powerful weapon against the devil. It's what the Lord used against the devil in his confrontation with him in the wilderness. He always answered him back with, "It is written."

One of the best ways to resist the devil and to put him to flight is to quote to him what's written in the Word of God. The Word of God on your lips will be used by the Holy Spirit as a sword against the devil. So when the devil attacks you wield the sword of the Spirit, which is the Word of God. Tell him what the Bible says about him and his fate. If you do so he will flee in terror.

The last important piece of armor I would like to look at is that of prayer and fasting.

In Ephesians chapter 6 verse 18 the Bible tells us to pray always with all prayer and supplication in the spirit, so prayer also is part of this spiritual armor.

One of the most effective ways to pray against the devil is to pray in the spirit or to pray in other tongues. The Bible says that when you speak in other tongues you are actually speaking mysteries unto God see 1 Corinthians chapter 14 verse 2. I believe that many of these mysteries or secrets are to do with the devil and what he is up to. When you pray in the spirit you start tackling some of these mysteries and secrets.

Also, in most cases the call to this type of prayer is done or initiated by the Holy Spirit. The Holy Spirit gives you the unction to pray.

The problem with many intercessors is that many are not sensitive enough to the Holy Spirit to respond to these prayer summons. Many intercessors pray for problems from their point of view instead of Gods point of view. They pray for actual problems that are in manifestation. Their prayers are therefore not preventive in nature.

I believe it does not serve any purpose, to pray against the devil after his finished doing havoc on his way back home when the damage has already been done. People need to pray against the devil before he manifests in the physical realm. Unfortunately, many people start dealing with the devil after he has stricken.

Jesus told Peter that the devil had asked to sift him like wheat and that he had prayed for him. It was these prayers of Jesus that managed to keep Peter a Christian despite his denial of Jesus. It's worth noting that Peter never knew that the devil had put him in his sight or that he was under attack. He was actually sleeping instead of taking authority against the devil. I believe the reason Peter did not know about this attack is that he was not that sensitive to the Holy Spirit as Jesus was.

Unless you learn to be sensitive to the Holy Spirit and respond to his prayer summons, you can never be an effective intercessor. You will only be praying for problems after they have happened, and in a sense your prayers will be too late. Only by depending on the help of the Holy Spirit will you be praying for problems before they unfold.

Now talking about the subject of fasting, this is probably one of the most misunderstood subjects in the body of Christ. Jesus said some demons (the stronger ones) may refuse to go away unless people pray and fast—see Mark chapter 9 verse 29. Many people, however, don't know why and when to fast. Fasting is mainly a weapon against the devil and demons.

Some believe that fasting is a way to arm twist God or that it causes God to hear us better. This is far from the truth. What actually causes God to hear and answer us is if we pray in accordance with his will.

The Bible says, "And this is the confidence that we have in him that if we ask anything according to his will he heareth us" (1 John 5:14).

It goes on to say in the next verse, "And f we know that he hear us whatsoever we ask we know that we have the petitions that we desired of him" (1 John 5:15).

God does not necessarily hear us because we have prayed for a long time or because we are praying very loudly. He does not necessarily hear us because we are fasting. The key to being heard and to receiving yes as an answer is praying in the will of God.

When we humble ourselves in fasting, however, we access more of the power of God to deal with demons. Secondly concerning fasting most people are used to what I call "appointed fasts."

In appointed fasts, the one fasting sets both the date and the time of the fast and when it's to end. This is the type of fast the religions of the world conduct. They determine beforehand when their fasts are to begin and end. The Jews conduct a similar fast every year on the Day of Atonement.

This is a very ineffective way to fast because surprise is a key element in the devil's attacks. The devil always loves to show up unannounced and when he is least expected. He may on purpose choose not to attack during your planned fast and do so just after you break your fast when you are too weak to start another one.

The Bible says that Jesus was led in the wilderness to be tempted by the devil. So Jesus never led himself in this forty-day fast. You need to be led by the Holy Spirit in your fasting. The Holy Spirit will always lead you to fast whenever it's necessary. When there is looming danger the Holy Spirit may lead you to fast. He weighs if it's necessary and advises you accordingly.

Not every demonic attack necessitates a fast. Sometimes you may put the devil to flight by just taking authority over him with the Word of God or by just rebuking him. Your duty is to sense the exact thing the Holy Spirit is leading you to do.

Some people say that they have to fast for forty days because Jesus, Moses, and Elijah fasted for this number of days. This is just being religious unconsciously.

The Bible says concerning the forty-day fast of Jesus that the Holy Spirit led Him to the wilderness to be tempted by the devil—see Matthew chapter 4 verse 1. So according to the scriptures the purpose of Jesus going to the wilderness and fasting for forty days was to avail the devil an opportunity to tempt him. The wilderness and the fast were a set up for this satanic temptation.

Jesus never went to the wilderness to get power against the devil as some people believe. He received this power when he was filled with the Holy Spirit, during his water baptism on the river Jordan.

I personally believe that it was the devil that requested to tempt Jesus after a forty-day fast. I believe the fast was requested by the devil in the first place. The Bible says the devil requested to tempt Job and also to sift Peter like wheat, so I would not at all be surprised that he was the one who put in the request for this temptation.

The Bible says that after the forty days of fasting Jesus was hungry, and that's when the devil came and started to tempt him—see Luke chapter 4 verses 2–3.

The devil likes to tempt us when we are most vulnerable. He chose to tempt Jesus when he was very hungry and starving after forty days of fasting. The forty-day fast was, therefore, a test of obedience while under stressful circumstances for Jesus and not to generate power, as some people believe.

This by implication means, that you put yourself in harm's way, if you just engage in long fasts without being led by the Holy Spirit because unlike Jesus, you may not have the stamina to endure tests in such a state of hunger. Actually Jesus taught us to pray that the Lord should not lead us into temptation for the simple reason that many would not be able to survive it.

The Bible also says that God does not bring temptation to us that we cannot bear or endure. So without following his guidance, you can bring upon yourself temptation you cannot endure by going on a prolonged fast. Yes, it's true that some fasting can move you from a fleshly position into a spiritual position where the anointing can flourish, but believe me this does not take forty days.

As for me, most of the time, it takes me hours to move from the flesh into "the spirit." A few other times when these demonic attacks were stronger, I have been led by the Holy Spirit to fast overnight or for two straight nights. I have, of course, led myself to fast longer than this due to a lack of knowledge. When you are fasting under the unction of the Holy Spirit, fasting is easy because the Holy Spirit empowers you to endure it. When, however, you are just in the flesh it becomes very burdensome, and you feel acute hunger.

A problem people face when fighting against the devil is the erroneous belief that they can get rid of the devil from their life for good. That's why some of them are attempting these marathon fasts. You can get rid of a demonic attack, but you can't stop completely having problems with the devil. The Bible says that after the temptation of Jesus in the wilderness the devil left him for a "season" implying that he came back after sometime to attack and tempt him.

When the disciples of John asked Jesus why his disciples never fasted, he responded that the time was coming when they were going to fast. He went on to say that you can't put new wine into old wineskins. This is because wine expands when it ferments; in so doing, it occupies a larger volume. So since the old wineskins have already expanded to their maximum limit, if new wine is put in them, the only option left is for the wineskins to burst when this wine ferments. If, however, you put the new wine into new wineskins, both expand simultaneously.

Jesus also said that you can't patch an old garment with a new piece of cloth because if you washed the garment the new piece would shrink, tearing the garment and making the hole larger. Jesus said that you needed to patch an old garment with an old piece of cloth.

Both of these illustrations were parables. What Jesus was putting across is that you cannot not just mix the new way of the gospel, grace, and salvation with the old religious way of Judaism.

The way we do things in this era of grace is different from the way they were done under the Law of Moses.

In this era of grace the emphasis is on being led by the Holy Spirit. Many times, unfortunately, we still hang on to the old way of doing things because we are so used to it. We pray and fast religiously. We give religiously and don't bother about the leading of the Holy Spirit. This is the reason why sometimes we never experience Gods miracles.

The Bible says that as many as are led by the Holy Spirit are the sons of God. The Holy Spirit wants to lead us in every arena of life. I have seen people who get saved and stay in their old religions find a lot of problems because mostly these two are not compatible. Certainly in the Bible this was a problem faced by the early church because some believers tried to mix Judaism with salvation and sometimes found contradictions.

God wants you to rise up and enter into your inheritance. We read in Obadiah, "... upon mount Zion shall be deliverance, and there shall be holiness; and the house of Jacob shall possess their possessions" (Obadiah 17). God wants you to possess that which belongs to you. Don't settle for anything less.

Law of Access

I would like to call the next law I want to discuss the law of access. This law says that you will only access that which you make contribution to. You can't access that to which you make no contribution.

The Bible says in the book of Proverbs, "a man's gift makes room for him and bringeth him before great men" (18:1). Here when the Bible talks of a gift, its talking about what we are actually giving, but your talent can also make room for you and bring you before great men. Our gift will give us access to those whom we are giving and even to other people. Our gift or what we contribute gives us favor and access to other people. Access is getting favor before others. It's being recognized by others.

We all need access at one time or another. I am sure we have all come across these signs that say that access is restricted or denied. Or those that say that only authorized personnel are permitted beyond certain points. We can get access through these restrictions, however, by using our gifts. Using our gifts will open for us doors that hitherto had been closed to us.

Look at King David. When he came to the battle-
field to bring his brothers food, he found Goliath, the
Philistine giant, challenging the children of Israel to a
fight one on one. When he used his gift of faith to slay
this giant (he surely had one), he received instant recognition by not only the royal house but also the entire
nation. Songs were composed in his honor. Jonathan took
off his garment and gave it to David. He became one of
the senior commanders in the army of Israel.

His gift made room for him and brought him before
great men. From being are nobody (his father also had
little regard for him and did not initially invite him to
parade before Samuel where he was to pick the next King
of Israel), he became an instant celebrity. I am sure every
young unmarried girl wished David to be their husband.
He got access into the royal palace and became the covenant friend of the crown prince, Jonathan, because he
made a contribution with his gift.

Look at Joseph when he used his gift of interpretation of dreams to interpret the king's dream and his gift
of wisdom to solve the problem of a looming famine. He
also became a great person overnight. He shot from being
a prisoner, to becoming the prime minister of all Egypt.
He now had access to the corridors of power in Egypt.

Look at Mordecai. He was driven on the king's camel
and dressed in the royal robes of the king because he
used his gift of uprightness to save the king's life. He
later became a prime minister in the land. He overheard
wicked men plotting to kill the king while he was sitting
at the gate and passed on the information to the king. He

could have chosen to keep silent because he was putting his life in jeopardy. The wicked men could have turned on him and killed him if the king did not believe him, yet his conscience could not allow him to keep quite. His gift made room for him and brought him before great men.

Look at the queen of Sheba when she came to visit Solomon:

> ... when the queen of Sheba heard of the fame of Solomon she came to prove Solomon with hard question at Jerusalem with a very great company. And camels that bare spices, and gold in abundance, and precious stone; and when she was come to Solomon she communed with him of all that was in her heart
>
> 2 Chronicles 9:1

Notice that the queen of Sheba never came empty handed to visit with Solomon. She came loaded with gifts. The Bible says, "... she gave the king a hundred and twenty talents of gold and of spices great abundance and precious stones: neither was there any such spice as the queen of Sheba gave King Solomon" (2 Chronicles 9:9). This made her welcome at King Solomon's court. It gave her access.

We read 2 Chronicles, "King Solomon gave to the queen of Sheba all her desire, whatsoever she asked, beside that which she had brought unto the King. So she turned and went away to her own land, she and her servants" (9:12). Her visit with King Solomon was a great success because she followed the law of access. She came with a gift, and it made room for her before King Solomon the greatest king on planet earth at the time.

Many people are looking at what they might receive from other people, not what they may contribute; that's why access is denied to them. Even Jesus gave a sacrifice of himself to get us access to the throne of God.

Why do you think Isaac asked his son Esau to prepare him his favorite dish before he could bless him? He wanted to help Esau access this blessing. He was going to now bless him with a joyful soul. The blessing was going to be genuine, coming from the bottom of his heart.

Why do you think Saul asked his servant whether they had a present for Samuel when they were going to him to inquire about their lost asses? See 1 Samuel chapter 9 verse 7. He knew the secret of the law of access.

If you want access, you don't go empty handed. Even with God, if you are in Jesus Christ and go with a sacrificial seed, you will find yourself getting access in areas that were hitherto inaccessible. Jesus Christ gives us the initial access, but this access can be enhanced with our sacrifices.

Many people who don't understand this law become critical when they hear people teaching along this line. They don't understand how your giving can make room for you.

In order for your gift or talent to make room for you and bring you before great men you have to first of all recognize it and then start using it. It's your key to getting access to the great places you desire to go. It's also very easy to recognize. What's your passion? What energizes you? What infuriates you when it's not done properly? Your answer to these questions can reveal your assignment and your gift.

God has given everyone a gift or a talent. You need to recognize your talent and use it in the right way diligently. I say the right way because some people are misusing their talent. Some people are using their God-given talent to glorify the devil instead of glorifying God.

Some people are not using their talents but are copying other people's talents. They think that the other people's talents are more profitable than theirs. This is a wrong notion because any talent can be profitable if put to use. Any talent can make room for you and bring you before great men. They are famous preachers, famous singers, famous chefs, etc. You don't need to adapt another person's gift in order to become a success.

Law of Greatness

I would like to call the next law I am going to discuss in this book, the law of greatness. This law says that the degree of greatness you will achieve will depend on the size of giant you kill. Your greatness is directly proportional to the size of giant you kill.

God is interested in us becoming great people on the earth. When he called Abraham, one of the promises he gave him was that he was going to make him great. In book of Genesis he told Abraham, "...I will make of thee a great nation, and I will bless thee and make thy name great and thou shall be a blessing" (12:2).

In the book of Deuteronomy, Moses told the nation of Israel that "and it shall come to pass, if thou shalt hearken diligently unto the voice of the Lord thy God, to observe and to do all his commandments which I command thee this day, that the Lord thy God will set thee on high above all nations of the earth" (28:1).

This is a promise of greatness God offers the nation of Israel. In verse 13 of the same chapter he goes on to say, "and the Lord shall make thee the head and not the tail; and thou shall be above only and thou shall not be beneath; if that thou hearken unto the commandments of the Lord thy God, which I command thee this day, to observe and do them" (Deuteronomy 28:13). All these are promises of greatness by God to his people.

God is interested in his people being great on the earth and doing mighty things. He does not want his people to be insignificant and helpless, just to be pitied by the world. He wants his people to do mighty exploits on the earth. He wants his people to build big hospitals and Universities. He wants us to build mega-church buildings, television and radio stations, etc.

King Solomon sent to Huram, the King of Tyre, and said,

> ... as thou didst deal with David my father and didst send him cedars to build him a house to dwell therein, even so deal with me. Behold I build a house to the name of the Lord my God, to dedicate to him, and to burn before him sweet incense and for the continual shew bread and for the burnt offerings morning and evening, on the Sabbaths and on the new moon and on the solemn feasts of the Lord our God. This is an ordinance for ever to Israel. And the house which I build is great for great is our God above all gods.
>
> 2 Chronicles 2:3–5

King Solomon wanted to build a great house for a great God. The Bible says, " ... the people that do know their God shall be strong and do exploits" (Daniel 11:32).

Greatness commands respect of the world. When you are great people will listen to what you have to say and take you seriously. You will be more effective in reaching out with the gospel when you are a great person. People will stop despising you and come to hear you out.

In the book of Genesis we read, "...and Abram was very rich in cattle, in silver, and in gold" (Genesis 13:2). He was not just rich; the Bible says he was very rich no wonder kings of the day respected him.

In Genesis chapter 14, verse 14, the Bible talks about 318 trained servants, who were born in Abraham's house. In Genesis chapter 14 verse 21–24 Abraham turned down the king of Sodom's offer for goods lest he should say he was the one who had made him rich. When I read these scriptures I start getting a feel of Abraham's greatness.

On an errand to get a wife for Isaac, Abraham's son, his servant testified to Abraham's future in-laws, "...and the Lord hath blessed my master greatly; and he is become great: and he hath given him flocks, and herds, and silver, and gold, and menservants and maid servants, and camels, and asses" (Genesis 24:35).

When his wife, Sarah, died, he refused a free offer of a plot of land to bury her and insisted on paying cash for it. Abraham was not only promised greatness, he actually obtained this promise of greatness in this life.

Even though Abraham had been promised this greatness, he had to kill several giants along the way, for him to enter into it. He had to kill the giant of childlessness in his home, even though he had passed the age of child-bearing and even though his wife was not only barren but had also passed the age of child bearing. This was a very big giant he had to kill no wonder he also won the undisputed title of "father of those who believe."

He had to kill another big giant of being ready at the request of God, to offer his son Isaac as a sacrifice to God. This was no small feat either. Even though God stopped him he counted it to have been done.

In book of Genesis God told him:

> ...by myself have I sworn saith the Lord, for because thou hast done this thing, and hast not withheld thy son, thine only son: That in blessing I will bless thee, and in multiplying I will multiply thy seed as the stars of the heaven and as the sand which is upon the seashore; and thy seed shall possess the gate of his enemies.
>
> Genesis 22:16–18

By killing this giant this time around, God swore an oath to bless and multiply him. At first he just promised by word of mouth, which is also sufficient because the Bible says it's impossible for God to lie, but because of the size of the giant killed by Abraham, God confirmed it with an oath. See Hebrews chapter 6.

David was a relatively an unknown shepherd boy looking after his father's sheep. Even his father did not regard him that much, because he never bothered to call him to the parade of his sons where Samuel was to pick a king, who was to replace King Saul, who had been rejected by God.

When, however, he single handedly slew Goliath the Philistine giant, he became an instant celebrity. He became a covenant friend of Jonathan the crown prince who "stripped himself of the robe that was upon him and gave it to David, and his garments, even to his sword and to his bow, and to his girdle" (1 Samuel 19:4).

He became a favorite of the king and started staying in the king's Palace. He became one of the army commanders and had bodyguards. He became the king's son-in-law, and his family was tax exempt.

Talking of greatness, David became one of the great people in Israel overnight. His finances shot up instantly. All this happened because he slew Goliath the Philistine giant.

You can achieve what others have taken years to achieve if you can only slay a giant. What I call a giant is something big, far bigger than you. If you can by faith achieve something great you are going to be listed in God's hall of fame.

The Bible says in the book of Daniel that the people who know their God will do exploits. An exploit is something big and spectacular. We serve a great God who is looking for people who are going to display his greatness to the world and bring him glory.

Many people are not on the road to greatness because instead of engaging giants, they are instead engaging insects. Many people are afraid to take on the giants and are saying that's not for me. Go in for the big catch if you want to enter God's greatness. Many of the children of

Israel failed to enter God's greatness in the promised land because they were afraid of the giants.

Are you facing a giant in your life? Don't back out. That's your ticket to greatness. The bigger the giant the greater you will become after slaying this giant. There are people killing giants all the time and are becoming greater and greater. These people are on worldwide television and are involved in big projects. Do you know why? The reason is because these people are not afraid to spend big bucks for Jesus. When you are only thinking about yourself and your family, there are people out there looking for big amounts of money to spend for the cause of Jesus. Why should God give you a million dollars if you are unwilling to spend this amount on him if the need arises?

To achieve greatness you must carry big dreams and have bold fearless faith. It takes bold faith to kill giants. When you are going in for the giants, you increase the stakes. The risks seem to increase. Giant killing is not for the faint hearted but pays big dividends. David put his life on the line when he went to confront Goliath. I am sure everyone held their breath as he was running to confront Goliath.

Sometimes it's the giants that can take on you like in the case of Joseph. He had to face the giant of being sold into slavery and of being imprisoned when he was innocent. His father, Jacob, while operating under the spirit of prophecy in Genesis, calls him "a fruitful bough even a fruitful bough by a well whose branches run over the well" (49:22).

He goes on to say, "... the archers have sorely grieved him and shot at him and hated him but his bow abode in strength and the arms of his hands were made strong by the hands of the mighty God of Jacob [from thence is the shepherd, the stone Israel]" (Genesis 49:22–24). He confronted big trials in his life that were really not of his own making. He passed through these trials with the right attitude, and God helped him overcome them. He later made it as prime minister of Egypt the greatest nation at the time. The bigger the giant you slay the greater you will become.

Daniel had, also like Joseph, to slay big giants in a foreign land as he rose to political prominence in Egypt. He put his life on the line by refusing to stop praying to God Almighty. He was thrown in a lion's den. God saved him from hungry lions and this made him even more prominent. He had to face the giants of confronting pagan Kings with the truth. These could order a death sentence any time.

You can also make it in Hebrews chapter 11, God's hall of fame. Just use your faith to slay a giant and your name will also appear there. Use your faith to achieve something big for God. Remember greatness always come with an attractive remuneration package like a nice house, a nice car etc.

Law of Success

I would like to call the last law I want to discuss in this book the law of success. This law says that if you are to succeed in this life you must purpose to walk in love toward everyone. The Bible says, "Charity [love] never fails" (1 Corinthians 13:8). If you want to avoid failure you have to determine to walk in love because it never fails. It always wins.

We must first of all discover the type of love we are talking about, because they are different types and the word *love* can mean many things to different people. The love I am talking about here is the *agape* love. This is the unconditional, God-kind of love that is described in 1 Corinthians chapter 13. We read in this chapter:

> Charity [love] suffereth long and is kind; charity envieth not; charity vaunteth not itself, is not puffed up, does not behave itself unseemly, seeketh not her own, is not easily provoked, thinketh no evil; rejoiceth not in iniquity but rejoieth in the truth; beareth all things, believeth all things,

hopeth all things, endureth all things. Charity never fails.

1 Corinthians 13:4–8

In this life, there will be many occasions of being offended. People will knowingly or unknowingly offend you, but if you want to succeed with your life you have to forgive them and move on. Jesus says in the Bible that offenses will inevitably show up. He says, "It is impossible but that offenses will come: but woe unto him, through whom they come" (Luke 17:10). Offense is part of this life, so you need to learn how to deal with it so that it does not hinder you. It's not a matter of if it comes; it's a matter of when it comes.

The Bible teaches that not walking in love is capable of hindering you. First of all it can hinder the operation of your faith. We read in the book of Galatians about "faith which worketh by love" (5:6). To put it bluntly, your faith will not work if you don't walk in love because faith works by love.

If someone stops your faith, he has cut off all your supplies, because we receive everything from God by faith, for "the just shall live by faith." Faith is a way of life and not a one day occurrence when we need a miracle in a certain area.

In the book of 1 Peter we read that "likewise, ye husbands, dwell with them according to knowledge, giving honor unto the wife as unto the weaker vessel, and as being heirs together of the grace of life; that your prayers be not hindered" (3:7). This is a sober warning to all of us especially the tough and mean husbands. Not walking in love can hinder your prayer life, another important life line we have with the Kingdom of God. You may pray and fast for God's help, but to no avail because you are not treating your wife correctly as the weaker vessel.

Jesus says, "And when you stand praying forgive if you aught against any: that your Father also which is in Heaven may forgive you your trespasses. But if ye do not forgive neither will your Father which is in Heaven forgive your trespasses" (Mark 11:25–26). So not walking in love can hinder our faith and our prayer life. It's one of the reasons why some people have long lists of unanswered prayers.

Joseph was very badly treated by his brothers. They wanted to kill him and later sold him off as a slave to the Ishmaelites who took him to Egypt. Later, as Potiphar's chief servant, he had some reprieve, but it was short lived. This time it was Potiphar's wife who got him in trouble because he refused to jump in bed with her. She falsely accused him of trying to rape her. An angry Potiphar threw Joseph in prison.

Life had more than once dealt a bitter blow to Joseph. He had every reason to become bitter and angry. The Bible says, however, that his "bow abode in strength and the arms of his hands were made strong by the hands of the mighty God of Jacob; from thence is the shepherd, the stone of Israel" (Genesis 49:24). He strengthened himself in God, and refused to be overtaken by hate and bitterness, that's why he eventually made it to the office of prime minister of all Egypt.

When his father died, his brothers thought that it was for fear of his father, that he had not taken revenge on them. They thought that now since their father had died, he was going to take his revenge on them. To their surprise he did not. Instead he told them that God used their action to work together for good, even though they had meant it for evil. Joseph's success story can be traced to his decision to walk in love in the face of great offence.

The Bible in the book of Isaiah mentions that Jesus in his passion "made intercession for the transgressors" (Isaiah 53:12). He on the cross while dying asked God to forgive his killers. Because of this among other things, God says, "I will divide him a portion with the great and he shall divide the spoil with the strong" (Isaiah 53:12).

Do you want to divide a portion with the great and the strong? Then you must purpose to walk in love toward everybody. If you want to succeed in this life, you must not permit bitterness to take root in your life. It will destroy you and hinder your success.

Many people have ruined their marriages, their jobs, and their friendships because they have allowed the root of bitterness to take hold of them. We are told in the book of Hebrews, "Looking diligently lest any man fail of the grace of God; lest ant root of bitterness springing up trouble you, and thereby many be defiled" (12:15). Bitterness will not only poison you but also those surrounding because you will transfer it to them.

When John the Baptist sent people to Jesus to inquire whether he was the one to come or should they wait for another, Jesus in his response mentioned that blessed is he who is not offended in him. I believe he included this in his response because he detected some desperation and impatience in the inquiry of John the Baptist.

John the Baptist was the one who had in the recent past declared boldly to the masses that Jesus was the one because he had seen the Holy Spirit descend upon him as a dove, a sign apparently God had had given him. He clearly never expected events to turn out the way they did. He never expected to end up in prison certainly not for that long. This started creating doubts and impatience in his life, that's why Jesus had to caution him not to take offence in him.

The Bible tells us to love God with all our heart, soul, and strength and to love other people as ourselves. It goes on to say that this is a summary of the law and the prophets. We should not take offence with God and should not keep offence with other people. The children of Israel took offence with God and his servants and were overcome in the wilderness. They were not able to enter the Promised Land and perished in the wilderness.

When we talk of walking in love, we are of course not talking only about the area of forgiveness. Walking in love will also restrain you from doing certain things, which are hindering people to succeed in life. You see when you walk in love you don't only consider how you feel about something but also how other people feel about that very thing. We are told in the book of Romans:

Owe no man anything, but to love one another: for he that loveth another has fulfilled the law. For

> this, thou shalt, not commit adultery, thou shalt
> not kill, thou shalt not steal, thou shalt not bear
> false witness, thou shalt not covet; and if there
> be any other commandment, it is briefly com-
> prehended in this saying, namely thou shalt love
> thy neighbor as thyself. Love worketh no ill to his
> neighbor: therefore love is the fulfilling of the law.
>
> Romans 13:8–10

Agape love is not about you but about your neighbor. It's about other people's feelings and opinions. The Bible says love worketh no ill to his neighbor.

Walking in love will for example restrain you from engaging in an extra marital affair, because your family and God will be devastated by this. Walking in love will also restrain you from taking a second wife for the same reasons. Many people in Africa, and I believe elsewhere else, are failing in life for taking more than one wife. Walking in love will restrain from doing shoddy work for your employer or customer. Walking in love will restrain you from sin because you will realize that this is offensive to God.

Sin caused Adam and Eve to fail. They were clearly walking out of love when they ate the forbidden fruit, since this would offend God. Sin is still the greatest cause of failure in the world today. Walking in love will restrain you from doing a host of other things.

They are some people who for instance may halt divorce proceedings, when they think more deeply on how their children and God will figure in all this. They may choose to reconcile their so-called "irreconcilable differences" rather than to raise their kids as bastards.

Walking in love will also cause you to bless others, causing you to be blessed, because it's more blessed to give than to receive. In my own life I have blessed people when they had nearly nothing and have seen them come back to me years later, after God has blessed them, to bless me back. Even though these people don't bless you back God will still find some other person to use to bless you back. So do you want to succeed in life? Purpose to walk in love, because walking in love is the key to success.

To contact author
(Phone) 256772954484